TWENTIETH CENTURY
INTERPRETATIONS
OF

THE CRUCIBLE

TWENTIETH CENTURY
INTERPRETATIONS
OF
THE CRUCIBLE

A Collection of Critical Essays

Edited by
JOHN H. FERRES

Prentice-Hall, Inc. *Englewood Cliffs, N.J.*

Library of Congress Cataloging in Publication Data

FERRES, JOHN H   comp.
  Twentieth century interpretations of The crucible.

  (Twentieth century interpretations) (A Spectrum
Book)
  CONTENTS: Introduction, by J. H. Ferres.—Witchcraft
and the Puritans, by G. L. Kittredge.—The meaning of
McCarthyism, by E. Latham. [etc.]
    1. Miller, Arthur, 1915–   . The crucible.
I. Title.
  PS3525.I5156C734   812'.5'2   72–4734
  ISBN   0–13–194860–1
  ISBN   0–13–194852–0 (pbk.)

Quotations from *The Crucible,* by Arthur Miller, are used by permission of
The Viking Press and International Famous Agency.

10   9   8   7   6

Prentice-Hall International, Inc. (*London*)
Prentice-Hall of Australia Pty., Ltd. (*Sydney*)
Prentice-Hall of Canada Ltd. (*Toronto*)
Prentice-Hall of India Private Limited (*New Delhi*)
Prentice-Hall of Japan, Inc. (*Tokyo*)

Contents

v

PART FOUR—*Viewpoints*

PART FIVE—*Additional Scene*

Introduction

by John H. Ferres

I

Nothing in Arthur Miller's early years indicated that he would one day be recognized as one of America's leading dramatists. Born in Harlem, New York City, on October 17, 1915, the son of Isidore Miller, a prosperous garment manufacturer, he demonstrated at school a greater aptitude for athletics than for the arts. Limiting his reading to books no weightier than *Tom Swift* and *The Rover Boys*, he "passed through the public school system unscathed" by learning.[1] Although he distinguished himself in a sense by failing algebra three times, his teachers did not remember him when he later achieved fame as a dramatist.

With the collapse of Isidore Miller's business during the Depression, the family moved to a smaller house in Brooklyn (one probably similar to the Loman home in *Death of a Salesman*). Like his father, Miller took work when and where he could find it upon graduation from high school. For the next two and a half years, and for an additional five years after graduation from college, he worked as common laborer, farmhand, warehouse clerk, waiter, factory worker, longshoreman, seaman, truck driver, and assistant fitter. The sense of actuality in many of his plays is attributable in large part to his wide experience as a wage earner. Furthermore, the appreciation gained in these years for the dignity of labor and the skillful use of tools helps explain Miller's practice of writing as many as a thousand pages to get a hundred that satisfy him and the craftsmanship that characterizes his best plays.

1. Arthur Miller, quoted in Stanley J. Kunitz, *Twentieth Century Authors: First Supplement* (New York: Wilson, 1955), p. 669.

Miller is not the first writer, of course, to turn a profit from the popular belief that the truly representative American artist should first prove himself a "regular fellow" by serving an apprenticeship in the school of hard knocks. In Miller's case, hard knocks succeeded in bringing about an intellectual awakening where high school had failed. He began to read Dostoyevsky and to wonder about the forces responsible for the economic conditions of the 1930s. After 1929, Miller could not believe "in the reality I saw with my eyes." He was filled with the same yearning he found in *The Brothers Karamazov* for some connection with the "invisible world of cause and effect, mysterious, full of surprises, implacable in its course." [2] His determination to discover the "hidden logic" of the times, and the fact that "they gave writing prizes there," [3] brought him to the University of Michigan to study journalism and playwriting. Two early dramatic attempts, *Honors at Dawn* (1936) and *No Villain* (1937), earned him the first of many awards.

Armed with a bachelor's degree and his awards, Miller returned to New York in 1938 to join the Federal Theater Project. Before his tragedy on the conquest of Mexico could be produced, however, the project died and the playwright found himself on relief. In the next few years, he wrote scripts for radio at $100 a script, married Mary Grace Slattery, whom he had met in college, fathered two children, and worked at various jobs to support his family. Rejected by the army for medical reasons, he was asked to visit a number of army camps in 1944 to gather material for a war-movie script, *The Story of G.I. Joe. Situation Normal* (1944) is his journal of that assignment. He received another award from the Theater Guild, this time for *The Man Who Had All the Luck* (1944), a play that introduces in embryonic form the principal themes of *All My Sons* (1947) and *Death of a Salesman* (1949), his major plays of the 1940s: the search for meaning in life and for dignity of self, and the psychological web of betrayal, guilt, and moral responsibility in a father–sons relationship. Readers of *The Crucible* find Miller's comment on *The Man Who Had All the Luck* equally pertinent to the later play: "The

2. Arthur Miller, "The Shadows of the Gods: A Critical View of the American Theater," *Harper's*, 217 (August 1958), 34–43.

3. Quoted in Edwin Seaver, ed., *Cross-Section* (New York: L. B. Fischer, 1944), p. 556.

play was an investigation to discover what exact part a man played
in his own fate." [4] In *Focus* (1945), the novel that follows *The Man
Who Had All the Luck,* Miller finds that the real evil of anti-Semitism lies in its insidious demand that a man surrender his judgment,
and hence his integrity, to institutionalized prejudice. Again the
parallel with *The Crucible* is clear.

Miller himself was to have his share of both well-deserved luck
and trouble in the period ahead. In ten years between 1947 and
1956, five of his most important plays—*All My Sons* (1947), *Death of
a Salesman* (1949), *The Crucible* (1953), *A Memory of Two Mon-
days* (1955), and *A View from the Bridge* (1956)—and an adaptation
of Ibsen's *An Enemy of the People* (1950) were produced, published,
and showered with the highest awards in the American theater. The
death of Eugene O'Neill in 1953 left Miller with only one rival, Tennessee Williams, for the distinction of being considered the most
gifted living American playwright. By 1954 he was indisputably the
most controversial. In that year the State Department refused
Miller a passport to attend the opening of *The Crucible* in Brussels
on the grounds that he was believed to be supporting the Communist movement. As the most casual reading of his plays makes clear,
Miller is a forthrightly liberal social thinker, especially in the areas
of politics and economics. In fact, before he became disillusioned
with it, socialism held some appeal for him; but he firmly denied
harboring any Communist sympathies. Nevertheless, in 1955 the
New York City Youth Board cancelled its contract with Miller for
a film script on juvenile delinquency in the city and went ahead
with an investigation of his political beliefs and associations.

The following year, just five days after the University of Michigan
had awarded him an honorary doctor's degree, the controversy regarding Miller's political views broke out anew when the House
Committee on Un-American Activities summoned him to appear
before it. Under interrogation, Miller declined to name suspected
Communist sympathizers at meetings he had attended nine years
earlier. His steadfastness before the committee, reminiscent of Giles
Corey in *The Crucible,* added fuel to the headlines that greeted his
marriage in the same year to the movie actress, Marilyn Monroe,

4. Arthur Miller, introduction to *Arthur Miller's Collected Plays* (New York:
Viking, 1957), p. 13.

shortly after divorcing his first wife—"Pinko Playwright Lands Love Goddess," etc. Additional fuel for the controversy was provided by Miller's well-publicized trial and conviction for contempt of Congress in 1957, a conviction later reversed by the United States Court of Appeals. Also in 1957 Miller's *Collected Plays* was published; it included an introduction by the author that is still considered an indispensable essay on modern drama and on Miller's evolution as a dramatist. For his achievement in the theater, Miller was elected to the National Institute of Arts and Letters and awarded its Gold Medal for Drama in 1959. It was not until 1961, however, that he was able to complete *The Misfits,* a film script written for Marilyn Monroe, thus breaking the writing drought that had begun with his political ordeal and second marriage. Miller's divorce from Miss Monroe came soon afterwards, and in 1962 he married Ingeborg Morath, a Swiss free-lance photographer.

For its opening in 1964, the Lincoln Center Repertory Theater in New York commissioned *After the Fall,* a dramatized examination-of-conscience by a disillusioned, guilt-ridden lawyer whose marital and political entanglements are obviously based on Miller's own life. Like *The Crucible* and Albert Camus's *The Fall* (1957), which it resembles in plot as well as title, *After the Fall* "is a trial; the trial of a man by his own conscience, his own values, his own deeds." [5] Its theme, the hero's loss of intellectual innocence, makes John Proctor, whose selfless martyrdom had seemed so redemptive to Miller a decade earlier, seem an implausible anachronism. As with *The Crucible* when it was first produced, interest in the play's surface—its tabloid subject and biographical details—sometimes prevented thoughtful consideration of its larger theme. As with *The Crucible,* too, Miller became involved afterward in a contretemps with the government when he declined to attend the ceremonial signing of the Arts and Humanities Act of 1965 because of his opposition to the war in Vietnam. In its second season, the Lincoln Center Repertory Theater staged Miller's long one-act play, *Incident at Vichy* (1964), which returns to the theme of persecution found in *The Crucible* and in *Focus,* specifically Nazi political persecution of Jew and Gentile alike in France during World War II. As in *The Crucible,* self-

5. Arthur Miller, "Foreword to *After the Fall,*" *Saturday Evening Post,* 237 (February 1, 1964), 32.

awareness and self-realization through commitment are the sine qua non of human existence, but this time the emphasis is on the silent complicity in persecution on the part of the persecuted and those professedly opposed to it rather than on the need for moral conversion or martyrdom.

Following publication of a collection of short stories, *I Don't Need You Any More* (1967), Miller returned to drama with *The Price* (1968), another family drama that analyzes, with evidently autobiographical overtones, moral responsibility and guilt in the relationship of two brothers. The connection is confirmed by Miller, who has said that "in terms of theme, I think the play is an outgrowth of *Death of a Salesman*." [6] Like *After the Fall* and *Incident at Vichy*, *The Price* suggests that the basic preoccupations of Miller's plays have deviated little from the course he charted some thirty years ago.

II

To many in the audience at the Martin Beck Theater in New York where it opened on January 22, 1953, *The Crucible* seemed to draw a parallel between the Salem witch trials of 1692 and government investigations of alleged Communist subversion in this country in the late 1940s and early 1950s. Given the national temper at the time, this is hardly surprising.[7] Henry Popkin reminds us that for several years before *The Crucible* was produced "public investigations had been examining and interrogating radicals, former radicals, and possible former radicals, requiring witnesses to tell about others and not only about themselves. The House Committee to Investigate Un-American Activities evolved a memorable and much-quoted sentence: 'Are you now, or have you ever been, a member of the Communist party?' Borrowing a phrase from a popular radio program, its interrogators called it 'the $64 question.' " [8]

6. Quoted in *The New York Times*, January 28, 1968, p. D-5.
7. In addition to picketing by various right-wing groups, the play was picketed by the American Bar Association for depicting the Puritan judges unsympathetically.
8. Henry Popkin, "Arthur Miller's *The Crucible*," *College English*, 26 (November 1964), 139.

Far from denying the parallel, Miller has emphasized it repeatedly in the interpolated commentary on *The Crucible,* in the introduction to the *Collected Plays,* and elsewhere, while insisting at the same time that he was really concerned with what lay behind the historical phenomena:

> It was not only the rise of "McCarthyism" that moved me, but something much more weird and mysterious. It was the fact that a political, objective, knowledgeable campaign from the far Right was capable of creating not only a terror, but a new subjective reality, a veritable mystique which was gradually assuming even a holy resonance. The wonder of it all struck me that so picayune a cause, carried forward by such manifestly ridiculous men, should be capable of paralyzing thought itself. . . . Astounded, I watched men pass me by without a nod whom I had known rather well for years; and again, the astonishment was produced by my knowledge . . . that the terror in these people was being knowingly planned and consciously engineered, and yet all they knew was terror. . . . There was a new religiosity in the air, not merely the kind expressed by the spurt in church construction and church attendance, but an official piety which my reading of American history could not reconcile with the free-wheeling iconoclasm of the country's past. I saw forming a kind of interior mechanism of confession and forgiveness of sins which until now had not been rightly categorized as sins. New sins were being created monthly. It was very odd how quickly these were accepted into the new orthodoxy, quite as though they had been there since the beginning of time. . . . I saw accepted the notion that conscience was no longer a private matter but one of state administration. I saw men handing conscience to other men and thanking other men for the opportunity of doing so.[9]

Later he was to write, "I thought then that in terms of this process the witch-hunts had something to say to the anti-Communist hysteria."[10]

Miller has attributed *The Crucible*'s relatively brief initial Broadway run of six months—*Death of a Salesman* ran for over eighteen —to the reviewers' dismissal of the play "as a cold, anti-McCarthy

9. Arthur Miller, introduction to *Collected Plays,* pp. 39–40.

10. Arthur Miller, "It Could Happen Here and Did," *The New York Times,* April 30, 1967, II, 17.

tract." [11] But with the exception of Brooks Atkinson and Walter
Kerr, the newspaper reviewers either denied or chose to ignore the
contemporary parallels, while generally praising the play itself. Eric
Bentley claimed that Miller had overlooked the crucial point that
Communism, as distinct from witchcraft, does in fact exist, but
praised his ability as a playwright. On the other hand, some reviewers had as many reservations about that ability as they did about the
parallel with McCarthyism. The first act was too diffuse, they said;
or the treatment of plot was too conventional after *Death of a Salesman*. A few years later the play was revived off-Broadway, where it
ran for over 500 performances to much more certain acclaim, and
since then it has been in almost continuous production in this
country and abroad. It held the stage for several seasons in France
and has found a permanent place in the repertories of such illustrious companies as Sir Laurence Olivier's National Theater in
Great Britain. Next to *Death of a Salesman,* it remains Miller's most
popular play in both the theater and the classroom.

III

The contemporary appeal of *The Crucible* can hardly be attributed to any analogy it draws between the Salem witch-hunts of 1692
and Joe McCarthy's Communist hunts, however, since the majority
of those who see or read the play today are probably too young to
remember the Wisconsin senator. Foreign audiences must be even
less conscious of the analogy. Why then has *The Crucible* held up
so well? What makes it still worth reading and performing? One can
perhaps begin to answer these questions by quoting something that
Miller said in an interview about his later play, *After the Fall*: "I
am trying to define what a human being should be, how he can sur-
vive in today's society without having to appear to be a different
person from what he basically is." [12] Despite its seventeenth-century
setting, he might have been talking about a central theme of *The
Crucible,* not only for audiences of the McCarthy years but for

11. Ibid.
12. Quoted in Kenneth Allsop, "A Conversation with Arthur Miller," *Encounter,* 13 (July 1959), 59.

those of today as well. Certainly the play more than bears out Miller's belief that drama is "the art of the present tense." [13]

To put it simply, Miller believes a man must be true to himself and to his fellows, even though being untrue may be the only way to stay alive. Out of the ordeal of his personal crucible, each of the principal characters comes to know the truth about himself. In order to confront his essential self, to discover that self in the void between being and seeming, a man must strip away the disguises society requires him to wear. John Proctor, refusing at the moment of truth to sell his friends, tears up his confession. Making a comparable decision, a character in *After the Fall* says, "Everything kind of falls away, excepting—one's self. One's truth." [14] Once the self has been revealed by this process, a man must be true to it. Much more than Proctor's era or the Cold War period, ours is a time when traditional values are eroding. The individual feels compelled to look inward for new ones. A man must either stand or fall alone once the fog of old standards has been burned away in the crucible of crisis. Stand or fall, though, he can achieve wholeness of being or "a sense of personal inviolability," [15] in Miller's words, that justifies new faith in himself.

The possibility of genuine self-awareness is a remote one for most people today—not so much because few are tested as Miller's characters are, but because few, to paraphrase Thoreau, are able to live deliberately and confront the essential facts of life. The concern of writers with the loss of the self in modern society has given rise to a whole literature of existential search for identity. It is precisely his identity, his "name," that Proctor will not surrender. The size, complexity, and diversity of our urban technological civilization, in alliance with Madison Avenue techniques for manipulating the mind and stereotyping the personality to a collection of consumer wants, make it difficult to identify the essential self beneath the layers of pseudoself. The real measure of Proctor's heroism as a standard for today lies in his ultimate discovery that life is not worth living if it must be preserved by lies told to one's self and one's friends.

---

13. Arthur Miller, introduction to *Collected Plays*, p. 11.
14. *After the Fall* (New York: Viking, Compass edition, 1964), p. 35.
15. Henry Hewes, "Arthur Miller and How He Went to the Devil," *Saturday Review*, 36 (January 31, 1953), 24.

Since self-understanding implies dissent, the spirit of dissent is strong in *The Crucible,* as strong perhaps as it was among the original Puritans. In the play, the word *authority* always means authority without inner sanction and always implies skepticism. Whether it ought to or not, Proctor's "I like not the smell of this 'authority' " (p. 28) [16] strikes a responsive chord at present. The struggle of Proctor and the others against the theocracy's repressive, irrational, and destructive use of authority is not without parallel in times more recent than the early 1950s. Proctor's gradual rejection of it is a paradigm of the intellectual misgivings of many today. He is shown first to be merely independent-minded about going to church. His excuse is that he needs the extra workday if his farm is to produce to capacity. We learn next that the real reason is his resentment of the Reverend Mr. Parris' grasping materialism, hypocritically concealed behind a façade of piety, and also his preoccupation with his congregation's possible future in hell instead of its actual spiritual needs in the present. Although Proctor has never "desired the destruction of religion" (p. 64), he can "see no light of God" (p. 63) in Parris and is "sick of Hell" (p. 27). His disillusionment is not complete, however, until he is arrested for witchcraft. At that point he is convinced that "God is dead!" (p. 115).

If not dead, then certainly He has withdrawn His blessing from a system engaged in persecutions worse than·the Anglican Church's persecution of the Pilgrims, from which they had sought refuge in the New World. Like many revolutionaries and reactionaries today, Danforth and Hathorne are convinced that since their cause—the extirpation of Satan and all his works from the new Canaan—is right and just, any means is justifiable in serving that end. Freedom of thought and expression, as well as a man's right to a fair trial, may therefore be denied, with the judges abrogating the most common-sense rules of evidence while they intimidate the community into accepting their self-serving view of justice. Proctor's questions, "Is the accuser always holy now?" (p. 74) and "Is every defense an attack upon the court?" (p. 89), are met by Danforth's "I cannot pardon these when twelve are already hanged for the same crime" (p. 124). Proctor is indeed attacking the court, and perhaps the whole system it represents, but his protest ends in frustration and what amounts

16. All page references are to *The Crucible* (New York: Bantam, 1959).

to suicide because the court itself insists on arbitrating the dispute.

Proctor rebels against the essentially totalitarian view of society that Danforth and Hathorne uphold. It is the view that the state knows best how a man should think and act. Carried to its extreme, as it was in the witchcraft trials, it bears out Nietzsche's dictum that the basis of society is the rationalization of cruelty. Proctor represents the view of society held by the Enlightenment thinkers—that society should be founded on the common good, as agreed upon by all reasonable men. This may be seen in his attitude toward adultery with Abigail. He feels guilt not so much because the Church has decreed adultery a sin as because it goes against "his own vision of decent conduct" (p. 18). Rather than an oppressively paternal state prescribing what he does, man needs a community whose essence is human, with friends who share common goals and beliefs. The witch trials demonstrate that the theocracy in effect suppresses the growth of such a community by inducing and finally forcing people to betray one another.

The position of the theocracy in 1692 was that witchcraft was both a sin and a crime, albeit an invisible one. Its very invisibility, however, showed it to be a phenomenon of great mystery and, as such, best dealt with by those qualified to deal with mysteries—namely, the civil and ecclesiastical officers of the theocracy. The Proctors, and finally Hale, want no part of mystery when a man is on trial for his life. Nevertheless, Americans are a people whose religious roots bind them to a belief in mystery. They are also a people whose traditions, both secular and religious, bind them to a belief in rationalism. Miller believes the American audience will side with Proctor in his encounter with Hale in Act I. When Hale arrives in Salem with armfuls of books on witchcraft, Parris takes some and remarks on how heavy they are. To Hale's reply that they are "weighted with authority" (p. 34), Proctor says that he has heard Hale is "a sensible man" (p. 35) and hopes he will leave some sense in Salem. The Puritans were the first Americans to experience our characteristic equivocation between belief in mystery, or myth, and faith in nonmystery, or rationalism. Dedicated by an unworldly religion to a life of self-denial and self-restraint as preparation for the mystery of heavenly salvation, they found themselves in a land eager to reward then and there material ambitions and appetites that were quite unmysterious in origin. Proctor, as noted earlier, cannot pass up the chance to get in an extra day's plowing on Sunday—any more than he can forgo his opportunity with Abigail.

The Salem episode can be seen as the inevitable explosion of a social schizophrenia suppressed for sixty years. To the extent that this condition was the product of real or imagined threats from outside the Puritan enclave, war with the pagan Indians or the French Papists might have been the result. But in fact the Salemite found exorcism of his schizophrenia in the hysteria of the witch trials and the sacrifice of the scapegoat victims. The Reverend Mr. Hale, comprehending at last the enormity of the witch trials, denounces them at the same moment that Proctor concludes God is dead. A churchman in conflict with the Church, a convert to humanism opposed to all he once epitomized, Hale denounces the theocratic system. Faced with a Church that will hang a person on the strength of a controversial passage of Scripture, Hale concludes that "Life . . . is God's most precious gift; no principle, however glorious, may justify the taking of it" (p. 127). One of these scriptural principles was the charitable obligation of each Christian to be his brother's keeper, a principle that in 1692 had been perverted to sanction malicious gossip and informing. If the witch trials marked the end of the theocracy's power in Massachusetts, it was because the theocracy had ossified into a monument to dead ideas as far as the John Proctors were concerned. As Miller notes, "the time of the armed camp had almost passed, and since the country was reasonably—although not wholly—safe, the old disciplines were beginning to rankle" (p. 3). In the play, the failure of the parents to see through the children's pretense of witchcraft is consistently ludicrous until it becomes tragic. Expecting children to behave as adults, the Puritans nevertheless refused to respect them as adults. In this way they assured rebellion against their authority, whether in the form of a childish prank that gets tragically out of hand, or the plain refusal of a Mary Warren to stand for whippings and being ordered to bed. "I am eighteen and a woman," she says (p. 58).

It must be said, in extenuation perhaps, that the Puritans believed in witchcraft much more firmly than they understood the natural penchant for mischief of the young, which could also be assigned to a diabolical source. Even had they understood, doubt-

less they would have felt that to dismiss the phenomenon before
their eyes as a childish prank was exactly what Satan wanted them
to do. They had no knowledge of child psychology, much less the
psychology of hysteria. Rebecca Nurse is the only one to state what
seems so obvious to us, but no one listens. A mother of eleven children, Rebecca has "seen them all through their silly seasons, and
when it comes on them they will run the Devil bowlegged keeping
up with their mischief. . . . A child's spirit is like a child, you can
never catch it by running after it; you must stand still, and, for love,
it will soon itself come back" (p. 24).

Part of the contemporaneity of *The Crucible* lies in its universal-
ity. The right of dissent versus the claims of authority makes up a
conflict as old as organized society. Both Sophocles' *Antigone* and
Shaw's *Joan of Arc* afford parallels to *The Crucible* in this connection. Names like Roger Williams, Anne Hutchinson, Henry David
Thoreau, Martin Luther King, and indeed the whole tradition of
minority dissent in America come to mind. The witch trials confront the mind with another age-old question too: how should we
respond to evil? And its equally ancient corollary: what if the evil
lie in us? Writing about *The Crucible* in 1967, Miller said:

> No man lives who has not got a panic button and when it is pressed
> by the clean white hand of moral duty, a certain murderous train is
> set in motion. Socially speaking, this is what the play is and was
> "about," and it is this which I believe makes it survive long after the
> political circumstances of its birth have evaporated in the public
> mind. [This] tragic process underlying the political manifestation
> [is] as much a part of humanity as walls and food and death, and no
> play will make it go away. When irrational terror takes to itself the
> fiat of moral goodness, somebody has to die.[17]

A susceptibility to paranoid fear is often the root of human
tragedy, whether manifested in the slaughter of the Biblical innocents or in the internment of one hundred thousand Japanese-
American citizens during World War II. In other words, if *The
Crucible* is a social play, it applies to all societies rather than to any
particular one. The setting of 1692 and the sociopolitical climate of
1953 take on the quality of timelessness found in Greek or Shake-

17. Arthur Miller, "It Could Happen Here and Did."

spearean tragedy. The persecution of both periods becomes the persecution of any period. But although Miller is careful to show how personal interest can infect society, the play seems less concerned now with a social condition than with a moral dilemma that continues to be part of the human condition for each one of us. In the same way, perhaps, *King Lear* is not, at least for modern readers, a tragedy about the social, much less the cosmic, effects of a king's misrule, but rather about the personal consequences of an old man's perversity for himself and his immediate circle.

For Americans, the play has something additional to offer in reminding us of our still potent Puritan legacy. It is a legacy larger in its effects than ever before because of the growth of America since the date of inheritance, although the passage of time has made it harder to recognize. As Miller points out, the Puritans believed that as God's chosen people they held "the candle that would light the world," and our inheritance of their belief has both "helped and hurt us" (p. 3). It provided much of the zeal and discipline necessary to civilize a new land and eventually make it into a Christian nation. It also degenerated into the imperialism of the Manifest Destiny doctrine in the nineteenth century in the same way that a crusade against Communism has degenerated, in the view of many, into military aggrandizement in this century. Danforth's black-and-white edict that one is "either with this court or he must be counted against it" (p. 90) is not very remote from either the continuing tendency of the conservative mind to regard foreign and domestic attempts at radical social transformation as conceived in Communism and born to subvert democracy, or the contrary tendency of the radical mind to suppose that to it alone has been vouchsafed the revelation of political and moral truth. If the use of violence is any indication, the Puritan psychology of terror is a national obsession that grows each year.

IV

From a literary standpoint, the best reason for reading or performing *The Crucible* today is simply that it is a good play. It has always been recognized as absorbing theater, with Miller's skill in sustaining excitement and suspense never in question. But the tendency among earlier critics was to overstress the defects that accompany these virtues. Certainly most of the clichés indispensable to courtroom melodrama are present in the trial and prison scenes. We learn virtually nothing of the background of even the major characters, and all of them fall too neatly into groups: those who grow morally, like the Proctors and Hale; those who remain static, like Danforth, Hathorne, and Abigail; and those who flounder somewhere in between, like Parris, Tituba, and the girls. It is a question, too, whether Proctor's guilt as an adulterer is not more of a box-office device than an adequate foundation for the larger implications of the play. Structurally, the action seems slow in getting under way because of the clutter of minor characters and the clumsiness of the exposition in Act I—a clumsiness the more surprising in view of Miller's awareness that exposition is "the biggest single dramatic problem." [18] The fourth act, too, omits the scene of confrontation between John and Abigail toward which the play has been building.[19] Once these concessions have been made, the play can hold its own.

To classify it as a morality play is to misread it badly. The Proctors, together with Giles Corey and Rebecca Nurse, have human failings that make their goodness more convincing, and Danforth and Hathorne, among the villains, are also men of conscience and principle. Their principles are not wrong simply because they are inflexible. One of the most baleful ironies in the play is that both Proctor and Danforth believe they are fighting against the same evils of irrationality and ambiguity in the administration of justice and against their anarchic influence. Locked into the "contention of the state . . . that the voice of Heaven is speaking through the children" (p. 84), Danforth must in conscience regard attacks upon the court as attacks upon God—which is to say the theocracy. Proctor is convinced the theocracy is an offense against God because it would deny the humanity of His creatures. (His equally stern conscience reflects a kind of secular Puritanism, as rigid and self-righteous in its way as Danforth's orthodox variety.) Although he must seem obtuse

18. Arthur Miller, introduction to *Collected Plays*, p. 21.
19. Miller added a confrontation scene (see "A Private Meeting of John and Abigail," p. 109) for a stage version produced in July 1953 but omitted it from later texts.

to us, Danforth does not know the trials are a fraud, as Proctor alleges he does; and it is conscience as well as egotism that virtually closes his mind to this possibility. He is fully aware that he has already condemned seventy-two people to death for witchcraft. And there is no evidence in the play that he is being hypocritical when he says he "will not deal in lies" (p. 138). It is noteworthy, too, that at least one critic of the court's methods plays fast and loose with the evidence himself. Giles Corey's "proof" that Putnam is conniving to gain a neighbor's property by having his daughter cry witch upon the neighbor is that Putnam admitted as much to an "honest man" who told Corey. Since Corey refuses, however, to name the man, he cannot be called to testify and the evidence remains purely hearsay.

Like many moderns, Proctor is himself suspicious of heroes and remains a reluctant and bewildered one until the last scene, when he embraces—as he believes—martyrdom. "He have his goodness now," says Elizabeth (p. 139), but earlier she had said he would have it anyway, whether he chose to die for truth or live a lie (p. 131). Hale thinks Proctor's death is vain and futile, but earlier Hale had said that if Proctor dies, "I count myself his murderer" (p. 126). Danforth, of course, feels the law has been correctly observed. It may be that in death, "goodness" is as ironic a word to apply to Proctor as he felt it to be in life. There is conceivably a double irony at work when Danforth tells Proctor in court that "we burn a hot fire here; it melts down all concealment" (p. 85). It may be that Miller is doing more than ironically foreshadowing Proctor's purification and the theocracy's ultimate disintegration in a crucible it intended for others. Perhaps he sees the task of creating and living up to one's own values, in the absence of absolutes, as beyond the capacity of even the John Proctors. Perhaps there *is* nothing left "to stop the whole green world from burning" (p. 69). There are overtones here of a theater of nihilistic despair.

As for belief in witchcraft, the characters cannot be easily classified as enlightened skeptics on the one hand and superstitious dupes on the other. Knowing their neighbors and themselves, the Proctors believe that the origin of the troubles in Salem is all too human. Yet they do not deny that witches exist, simply that there are any in Salem. And as Miller says, "Danforth seems about to conceive of truth." [20] The girls regard witchcraft as "sport," but Abigail does choke down some chicken blood, believing in its power to kill Elizabeth. It may be, too, that in Act I Betty Parris is not merely dissembling, but in a state of shock and fearful guilt after the escapade of the previous night. Some students of witchcraft have even maintained that witches were in fact abroad in Salem, in the sense in which the term was understood, and also that the judges conducted the trials with admirable caution and restraint considering this fact.[21] Given the common belief in witchcraft, which the girls may have shared, it is possible that any inclination to nervous instability combined with suspected malice in others could have produced the psychosomatic effects found in Betty and in Ruth Putnam. Similarly, in the superstitious society of the Australian aborigine, a scapegoat may become paralyzed and eventually die as a result of the psychological terror induced by the witch doctor's pointing a bone at him.

The language of the play should also be remarked. Miller has received consistently poor marks for the leaden realism of the dialogue in his other plays. In this, his first "history play," he has again chosen prosaic characters, but their historical remoteness allows him to use a semiarchaic language whose stark, rough eloquence lends the drama much of the immediacy of the realistic mode. The language is a means of escaping the bonds of conventional dramatic realism at no sacrifice of strength. On the whole the attempt is successful, since the language not only avoids the extremes of melodrama inherent in the playwright's subject, but fuses feeling and awareness in a way that had previously eluded him. Biblical-sounding, seventeenth-century speech rhythms often serve to charge events with a momentous, awesome significance, and at the end lift the language to the agonized lyricism of the speeches of the Proctors and Hale. Like the mind of its hero, the play's language is informed by a "heightened consciousness" [22] that can manifest a much greater degree of self-awareness on the part of the characters than can the tortured rhetoric of Joe Keller, Willy Loman, or Eddie Carbone.

20. Arthur Miller, introduction to *Collected Plays*, p. 43.
21. See, for example, Chadwick Hansen, *Witchcraft at Salem* (New York: Braziller, 1969).
22. Arthur Miller, introduction to *Collected Plays*, p. 53.

It seems appropriate, in conclusion, to focus on a scene that illustrates most of the dramatic qualities discussed above. The last scene of Act III constitutes the turning point in the action for the principal characters and brings together the main thematic concerns of the play. Danforth has just sent for Abigail and her girls in order to confront them with Mary Warren's deposition admitting they were merely pretending to be tormented by witches. Since Mary's deposition was actually written by Proctor, however, Danforth doubts its authenticity. He suspects Proctor of trying to destroy the authority of his court. In light of the deposition, Danforth suggests to Abigail that the spirits she has reported seeing may be illusory. She indignantly denies this and, feeling her efforts to supply the court with victims are insufficiently appreciated, hints that Danforth himself may not be above suspicion. The deposition having failed, Proctor concludes that the only way to discredit Abigail is to reveal their adultery and assert that the witchcraft hysteria is in reality a "whore's vengeance" directed at Elizabeth. "She thinks to dance with me on my wife's grave" (p. 106). Since Proctor says his wife knows of his "lechery," Danforth seizes the opportunity to discover the truth promptly. He has Elizabeth brought in for questioning, believing that because of her reputation and the Puritan belief in eternal damnation for those who bear false witness, she will not lie. To Proctor's horror, however, she tells the court that he is not a lecher. Another surprise follows when Hale comes to Proctor's defense. This in turn prompts a new outbreak of hysterics from Abigail and her chorus, the calculated frenzy of which is enough to cause Mary, already close to hysteria from Danforth's fierce interrogation, to abandon sanity once more and accuse Proctor of conspiring to overthrow the court. After Proctor is arrested, Hale denounces the proceedings and quits the court.

For each of the three principal characters, the trial scene represents a personal crucible of self-discovery through commitment. In defense of truth, Proctor discovers that he is willing to sacrifice his reputation and go to jail to save his wife. To save her husband, Elizabeth places loyalty and charity above literal truth and discovers the depth of her love for him. Hale also discovers that, ultimately, principles are less important than the preservation of human life. In each case, self-discovery carries bitterly ironic implications. With

Proctor it is the existentialist irony that a man may play a part in his own fate—thus gaining self-respect—if he is willing to lose his name, the respect of his neighbors, and possibly his life. Elizabeth's lie, probably her first and only, comes at a time when telling the truth has never been more important. Her ignorance of this, coupled with the audience's awareness, produces a clear example of tragic irony. Hale's moral conversion occurs only after he has signed seventy-two death warrants. Partly because of his refusal to surrender his conscience to the state, partly because of the confession forced out of him, Proctor achieves a measure of inviolability. Further, under the critical heat of the crucible-trial, the dross of old values and standards has burned away. The act of choosing new ones constitutes not only the discovery and justification of the self, but proof of its freedom as well.

As the exposition above implies, several personal and ideological conflicts of the play reach their climax in the trial scene. The personal conflicts include a Puritan version of the eternal triangle involving Abigail, John, and Elizabeth; the immediate conflict between John and Abigail concerning Mary's allegiance; and the open bitterness between Parris and Proctor over the former's fitness to be minister of Salem. More important are the suspenseful conflicts within the characters themselves. Should Proctor confess adultery in order to save a wife who virtually drove him to it? Should Elizabeth jeopardize her soul by lying to save a husband she believes feels "softly" still toward his former mistress? At the most basic level, the ideological conflict scarcely deserves the name. It is a bewildering confrontation between fanaticism and common sense. To tell the plain truth is to invite hanging; to "confess" is to win acquittal but invite damnation. In any case, evidence counts for nothing in this court because the judges believe only what they want to believe. The central and timeless ideological conflict, reflected in all the others, opposes the authoritarian state to the integrity of private conscience. The increasing doubts of Proctor and Hale regarding the theocratic system as represented by Danforth, Hathorne, and Parris finally explode into total repudiation. Miller makes clear that dissent is an obligation rather than a right when the individual is confronted with irrational, invidious, and repressive authority as manifested in the conduct of the witch trials. Hale comes to suspect that the confidence of the judges in their God-given ability to divine the truth is an absurd delusion stemming from an obsession with saving face for the theocracy at any cost. Miller is depicting a society in moral crisis, and through character, situation, and mood he unmistakably evokes contemporary parallels. Specifically, the play is at its most powerful in this scene because the playwright is dramatizing with clean precision the process by which psychological terror in the service of a clear and present evil may paralyze the collective mind and will of society.

Finally, the trial scene makes skillful use of the trusted conventions of courtroom melodrama. Miller contrives to keep the excitement mounting toward the hysterical climax through accusation and counteraccusation, startling confessions, hatreds vented, and lies shrewdly exposed. The scene also illustrates, at a deeper level, Miller's statement concerning the structure of *The Crucible*: ". . . the central impulse for writing at all was not the social but the interior psychological question . . . of the guilt residing in Salem which the hysteria merely unleashed, but did not create. Consequently the structure reflects that understanding, and it centers in John, Elizabeth, and Abigail." [23] After simmering beneath the surface for the first half of the play, the interlocking private guilts of these three erupt in public revelation under the pressure of the witchcraft hysteria. A personal guilt she will not accept is the real motive behind Abigail's irresponsible attempts to destroy Elizabeth by exploiting the Puritan phobia of witchcraft. Accepted guilt, as well as a desire to destroy Abigail, then leads to public confession and responsible acceptance of the consequences on Proctor's part. Guilt causes Elizabeth to betray John with the one genuine act of penance in the play.

23. Ibid., p. 42.

PART ONE

Background

Witchcraft and the Puritans

by George L. Kittredge

. . . The darkest page of New England history is, by common consent, that which is inscribed with the words Salem Witchcraft. The hand of the apologist trembles as it turns the leaf. The reactionary writer who prefers iconoclasm to hero-worship sharpens his pen and pours fresh gall into his inkpot when he comes to this sinister subject. Let us try to consider the matter, for a few minutes, unemotionally, and to that end let us pass in review a number of facts which may help us to look at the Witchcraft Delusion of 1692 in its due proportions—not as an abnormal outbreak of fanaticism, not as an isolated tragedy, but as a mere incident, a brief and transitory episode in the biography of a terrible, but perfectly natural, superstition.

In the first place, we know that the New Englanders did not invent the belief in witchcraft. It is a universally human belief. No race or nation is exempt from it. Formerly, it was an article in the creed of everybody in the world, and it is still held, in some form or other, and to a greater or less extent, by a large majority of mankind.

Further, our own attitude of mind toward witchcraft is a very modern attitude indeed. To us, one who asserts the existence, or even the possibility, of the crime of witchcraft staggers under a burden of proof which he cannot conceivably support. His thesis seems to us unreasonable, abnormal, monstrous; it can scarcely be stated in intelligible terms; it savors of madness. Now, before we can do any kind of justice to our forefathers—a matter, be it remembered, of no moment to them, for they have gone to their reward, but, I take it, of considerable importance to us—we must empty our heads of all such rationalistic ideas. To the contemporaries of William Stoughton and Samuel Sewall the existence of this crime was not merely an historical phenomenon, it was a fact of contemporary experience. Whoever denied the occurrence of witchcraft in the past was an atheist; whoever refused to admit its actual possibility in the present was either stubbornly incredulous, or destitute of the ability to draw an inference. Throughout the seventeenth century, very few persons could be found—not merely in New England, but in the whole world—who would have ventured to take so radical a position. That there had been witches and sorcerers in antiquity was beyond cavil. That there were, or might be, witches and sorcerers in the present was almost equally certain. The crime was recognized by the Bible, by all branches of the Church, by philosophy, by natural science, by the medical faculty, by the law of England. I do not offer these postulates as novelties. They are commonplaces. They will not be attacked by anybody who has even a slight acquaintance with the mass of testimony that might be adduced to establish them.

It is a common practice to ascribe the tenets of the New Englanders in the matter of witchcraft to something peculiar about their religious opinions—to what is loosely called their Puritan theology. This is a very serious error. The doctrines of our forefathers differed, in this regard, from the doctrines of the Roman and the Anglican Church in no essential—one may safely add, in no particular. Lord Bacon was not a Puritan, yet he has left his belief in sorcery recorded in a dozen places. James I was not a Puritan, but his Dæmonologie (1597) is a classic treatise, his zeal in prosecuting Scottish sorcerers is notorious, and the statute of 1604 was the act under which Matthew Hopkins, in the time of the Commonwealth, sent two hundred witches to the gallows in two years—nearly ten times as many as perished in Massachusetts from the first settlement to the beginning of the eighteenth century. . . .

The Salem outbreak was not due to Puritanism; it is not assignable to any peculiar temper on the part of our New England ancestors; it is no sign of exceptional bigotry or abnormal superstition. Our forefathers believed in witchcraft, not because they were Puritans, not because they were Colonials, not because they were New Englanders—but because they were men of their time. They shared the feelings and beliefs of the best hearts and wisest heads of the seventeenth century. What more can be asked of them? . . .

Another point requires consideration if we would arrive at a just judgment on the Salem upheaval. It is frequently stated, and still oftener assumed, that the outbreak at Salem was peculiar in its virulence, or, at all events, in its intensity. This is a serious error, due, like other misapprehensio..s, to a neglect of the history of witchcraft as a whole. The fact is, the Salem excitement was the opposite of peculiar—it was perfectly typical. The European belief in witchcraft, which our forefathers shared without exaggerating it, was a constant quantity. It was always present, and continuously fraught with direful possibilities. But it did not find expression in a steady and regular succession of witch trials. On the contrary, it manifested itself at irregular intervals in spasmodic outbursts of prosecution. . . .

There was a very special reason why troubles with the powers of darkness were to be expected in New England—a reason which does not hold good for Great Britain or, indeed, for any part of Western Europe. I refer, of course, to the presence of a considerable heathen population—the Indians. These were universally supposed to be devil-worshippers—not only by the colonists but by all the rest of the world—for paganism was held to be nothing but Satanism. Cotton Mather and the Jesuit fathers of Canada were at one on this point. The religious ceremonies of the Indians were, as we know, in large part an invocation of spirits, and their powwows, or medicine men, supposed themselves to be wizards—*were* wizards, indeed, so far as sorcery is possible. The colonial government showed itself singularly moderate, however, in its attitude toward Indian practices of a magical character. Powwowing was, of course, forbidden wherever the jurisdiction of the white men held sway, but it was punishable by fine only, nor was there any idea of inflicting the extreme penalty—although the offence undoubtedly came under the Mosaic law, so often quoted on the title pages of books on witchcraft, "Thou shalt not suffer a witch to live."

The existence of all these devil-worshipping neighbors was a constant reminder of the possibility of danger from witchcraft. One is surprised, therefore, to find that there was no real outbreak until so late in the century. It argues an uncommon degree of steadiness and common sense among our forefathers that they held off the explosion so long. Yet even this delay has been made to count against them, as if, by 1692, they ought to have known better, even if they might have been excusable some years before. In point of fact, the New Englanders, as we have seen, made an end of trying witches nearly twenty years earlier than their English fellow citizens. . . .

Much has been written of the stupendous and criminal foolishness of our ancestors in admitting "spectral evidence" at the Salem trials. Nothing, of course, can be said in defence of such evidence in itself; but a great deal might be said in defence of our ancestors on this score. The fact is—and it should never be lost sight of—there was nothing strange in their admitting such evidence. It was a matter of course that they should admit it. To do so, indeed, was one of the best established of all legal principles. . . . On the other hand, it is much to their credit that they soon began to suspect it, and that, having taken advice, they decided, in 1693, to allow it no further weight. . . .

The most remarkable things about the New England prosecution were the rapid return of the community to its habitually sensible frame of mind and the frank public confession of error made by many of those who had been implicated. These two features, and especially the latter, are without a parallel in the history of witchcraft. It seems to be assumed by most writers that recantation and an appeal to heaven for pardon were the least that could have been expected of judge and jury. In fact, as I have just ventured to suggest, no action like Samuel Sewall's on the part of a judge and no document like that issued by the repentant Massachusetts jurymen have yet been discovered in the witch records of the world. . . .

The Meaning of McCarthyism

by Earl Latham

. . . Senator Joseph R. McCarthy became a focus of the uproar over Communists in Federal employment. In February 1950, he charged that the Department of State knowingly harbored Communists, and for months the press was filled with the acrimony of the argument that ensued. In this verbal combat with the State Department and others, Senator McCarthy quickly established the style of contention that was to be admired (or condoned) by his supporters and to be deplored and even feared by his opponents, a style of which the principal elements were recklessness in accusation, careless inaccuracy of statement, and abuse of those who criticized him. Hearings on the McCarthy charges were held under the chairmanship of Senator Millard Tydings of Maryland, whose committee exonerated the State Department. Critics called the proceedings a "whitewash."

Other events of 1950 illustrate the force of the new fury over the Communist issue. The Supreme Court upheld the conviction of the eleven top leaders of the Communist Party under the Smith Act of 1940. The Court also refused to review the convictions of two Hollywood writers who had declined to answer questions about possible Communist connections. Judith Coplon of the Department of Justice was convicted of conspiracy with a Soviet representative at the United Nations (later reversed on procedural grounds). Harry Gold, David Greenglass, and Julius and Ethel Rosenberg were arrested on various charges connected with atomic espionage. A grand jury brought indictments against individuals involved in the transfer

of hundreds of secret and other classified documents from the State
Department to the offices of a relatively obscure journal called
Amerasia.

The storms of controversy blew just as hard for the next two years.
Early in 1951, the McCarran subcommittee seized the files of the
Institute of Pacific Relations and began a long investigation into the
relations between the Institute and the Department of State, relations which were thought to involve subversion. The Rosenberg
trial opened in March, and in April the Rosenbergs were sentenced
to death. The head of the FBI assured Congress that his organization was ready to arrest 14,000 dangerous Communists in the event
of war with the Soviet Union. A foundation offered $100,000 to sup-
port research into the creation of a device for detecting traitors.

At the beginning of 1952, Senator William Benton of Connecti-
cut tried to have the United States Senate expel Senator McCarthy.
In April, Senator McCarthy offered a resolution for a full-scale investigation into Senator Benton's official, business, and personal activities. In the presidential campaign in the fall of 1952, the Communist issue was given greater prominence than it had had in 1948.
Richard Nixon said that Adlai Stevenson had disqualified himself
for the presidency by providing a character reference for Alger Hiss
at the latter's trial for perjury. Twenty-two prominent lawyers, some
of them Eisenhower supporters, upheld Stevenson. Sixteen other
lawyers issued a statement contradicting the position taken by the
twenty-two. General Eisenhower accused the Administration of having permitted spies of the Soviet Union to steal secrets. Senator
McCarthy made a widely advertised television speech in which he
used "Alger" for "Adlai" in faked mistake. Although the change of
regime that was voted in 1952 was impelled by deeper forces than
the rhetoric of the national campaign, "Communism" was certainly
one of the symbols under which it occurred.

The first year of the Eisenhower era saw McCarthy at his peak. In
the second he was brought down and condemned. In 1953, Senator
McCarthy, now chairman of the Senate Government Operations
Committee, conducted an investigation of the Voice of America and
the overseas information programs of the State Department with
destructive roughness. Although he had no diplomatic credentials,
he negotiated an agreement with Greek ship owners about trade

with Communist China. He conducted a search for spies in the Signal Corps and the Fort Monmouth laboratories. In these highly publicized enterprises he had the volunteer assistance of unidentified employees in the Federal agencies who violated their trusts to supply him with information about their colleagues and superiors.

Eventually military and civilian officers of the Pentagon came to feel that he was intolerable, and they resisted further pressure from him and his staff. This resistance led to mutual charges and recriminations, and a special Senate committee was appointed to investigate the truth of the contradictory allegations. The committee merely aired and did not settle the controversy. In August 1954, Senator Ralph Flanders of Vermont introduced a resolution to censure McCarthy for his conduct, and hearings were held under the chairmanship of Senator Arthur Watkins of Utah. The Watkins committee found that Senator McCarthy had wrongfully defied the authority of the Senate and certain of its committees, and that he had been abusive of his colleagues (one he had called "a living miracle, without brains or guts"). After the fall elections of 1954, the Senate condemned McCarthy for these delinquencies.

From 1950 to 1954, the activities of Senator McCarthy were an oppresive weight and pain to tens of thousands in government, politics, and the professions specifically, and within the articulate and better educated circles of society generally. In America and abroad he became a symbol of mortal danger to liberal values and democratic processes. . . .

PART TWO

Reviews

Miller's *The Crucible* as Event and Play

by John Gassner

Jed Harris' Broadway production of *The Crucible*, Arthur Miller's drama of the Salem witchcraft trials, was received with qualifications. The play was not fully successful even after the touring version was restaged by the author. Only an off-Broadway production several years later seemed to do full justice to the play.

With the writing and production of *The Crucible* Miller moved in the directions that had already attracted him (he had written an unproduced poetic tragedy on the conquest of Mexico): history and tragedy. History was directly present in *The Crucible*, and tragedy was scaled higher than it had been in *Death of a Salesman*. His independent Colonial farmer, John Proctor, had more tragic stature than the superannuated traveling salesman, Willy Loman. The heroic death of Proctor, who chooses the gallows in preference to submission to unjust authority, is on an obviously higher level of tragic sacrifice than Willy's suicide.

We may surmise that Arthur Miller entertained poetic aspirations. Apparently he was following Maxwell Anderson's example in trying to write poetry in an historical drama before using it in a contemporary context (this came later in *A View from the Bridge*). The poetry in *The Crucible* was a sort of prose-poetry rather than verse, and the seventeenth-century historical context in which it was employed justified a degree of formality and biblical austerity. Miller was not the man to hit upon poetic embellishments accidentally; his play-

---

"Miller's The Crucible *as Event and Play." From the chapter "Affirmations?" in John Gassner,* Theatre at the Crossroads *(New York: Holt, Rinehart & Winston, Inc., 1960), pp. 274–78. Copyright © 1960 by Mollie Gassner. Reprinted by permission of the publisher.*

writing career appears to follow a planned progression from the
well-made-play technique of *All My Sons* to the imaginative dramatic construction of *Death of a Salesman* and to the poetic historical writing of *The Crucible*. The author's various introductions to
his plays make plain the deliberateness, the strong awareness of ob-
jectives, and the self-awareness that characterize his work in the
theatre.

The Crucible, then, has importance in the career of a writer whose
laudable ambition is to make contemporary American theatre aim
high and who also wishes to express the tensions of his own time and
place. Taking an exalted view of the theatre's responsibilities and of
the artist's function in society as the guardian of its conscience, Miller wrote *The Crucible* in the midst of the McCarthy era. The author's motivation plainly included taking a public stand against
authoritarian inquisitions and mass hysteria. These are pompous
words perhaps. The play itself has a little too much pomp at times
that better dramatic poetry might have transfigured, and too much
stiffness that the author might have avoided had he dealt with his
own times and been less conscious of period. But the sincerely maintained purpose behind the posture is clear, and it is one of Miller's
distinctions that he was one of the very few writers of the period to
speak out unequivocally for reason and justice. *The Crucible* will
remain alive long after every carping criticism directed at its political
implications has been forgotten. (Curiously, these criticisms were
not by benighted reactionaries but by enlightened intellectuals, and
not in the popular press but in literary journals.)

There were some dramatic rewards available to a person of Miller's courage. The topical incitement to passion gave the author a
strong impetus in the writing of the climactic scenes. These have
since been rarely equalled in strength, and the excitement they provided proved distinctly serviceable when the play was given an off-
Broadway revival in 1958, after McCarthyism had subsided as an
issue. The later production proved that the play could hold its own
without the support of topicality. That it stood up so well was due
to the excitement of the action, to the author's underlying passion,
and to the character drama and tragic pattern. All this does not
mitigate a certain stiffness in the characterization, nor does it remove
doubt as to the advisability of making the historical witchcraft trials

hinge so much on the perversity of a passionate girl. But the fact remains that Miller built his play with exciting situations and characters rather than puppets.

The Crucible was momentous, if imperfect. I give my own reactions below as a specimen first reaction to the play and its reception. At the second night opening, during the 1952–53 season, the strong impression on the audience was almost the impact of an *event* rather than of just one more serious play. Even while aware of some creakiness in the work, I shared a feeling of grief and anger with others. Writing about the play several weeks later, I had some doubts about the quality of the work. Yet I also wrote with some rage directed not only at the historical world of Salem, but at the evil and stupidity in men as well as at the frosty and what seemed to me at the time disingenuous reaction of various intelligent theatregoers:

> A History play by virtue of its subject, *The Crucible* is nonetheless a spiraling drama. Miller has once more demonstrated his ability to telescope dramatic material. In writing about the Salem witchcraft trials he has avoided the danger of composing a sprawling chronicle. Moreover, he has made every effort to create a central tragic character in John Proctor, the independent farmer who faces one decision after another and, after some understandable hesitations, makes his choice. It would take too long to prove here the proficiency combined with insight into character that distinguishes *The Crucible*. Even the painstaking Jed Harris production failed to capture the movement toward tragedy and toward unity through character drama Miller developed in his script. This achievement can be observed in the published Viking Press text.
>
> How the contemporary higher criticism can tie itself up in knots when it is confronted by honest, forthright work is well shown in reviews of the play. As usual, the workaday New York newspaper reviewers come off better than the critics who write for recondite publications; the newspapermen report on what they see, whereas esoteric critics see only what they want to discuss. Regardless of Miller's original intentions or later explanations in the Viking book, the play must be assessed simply as a play. If parallels between the past and the present appear, so much the worse for us or for humanity at large rather than for the playwright. If individual lines, such as the question whether the accuser is now always holy, are relevant and probably intentional on Miller's part, the fact remains that a

play that holds audiences in its grip as *The Crucible* does, succeeds
through the power of its overall dramaturgy rather than through its
topical features.

If there are obvious weaknesses in the play, they result mainly
from the fact that Proctor and his wife are swamped by such a mul-
tiplicity of secondary characters that the personal drama of maintaining integrity in the face of compounded evil and folly is often
dissipated. It is also unfortunate that the tragedy is started and
brought to a climax—and therefore made melodramatic—by the will-
ful action of a demoniacal girl, Abigail. Miller does not succeed in
overcoming these defects. But he appears to be aware of them, and
his awareness results in adjustments or corrections as the play pro-
ceeds. Both Proctor and his wife are made to grow in stature; at the
end they are fully developed. Perhaps they grow too rapidly in act
four of the text, and the Jed Harris production blurred this growth.
By the time the play ends, it is no longer the hit-or-miss chronicle of
mass hysteria it tended to become earlier; it is a tragedy and its
point is that men, no matter how erring, are capable of enduring
everything for their sense of decency. This, too, is more apparent
in the published text than it was in the stage production. Those
who claim that *The Crucible* is inadequate as a revelation of what
happened in Salem are quite correct. It is what transpired in the
souls of John and Elizabeth Proctor that finally matters, and to that
degree *The Crucible* is neither an exposé nor a merely contemporary
protest, but a tragedy. It is regrettable that Jed Harris did not succeed in bringing this out sufficiently in the performances of Arthur
Kennedy and Beatrice Straight. They were less commanding on the
stage than Walter Hampden's formidable Deputy-Governor Danforth. [A uniformity of excellence in the acting of the principals such
as in the off-Broadway 1958–59 Hotel Martinique production would
have called more attention to the personal tragedy that Miller came
to favor in the play.]

The fact is that good as the Broadway production was, it failed to
develop fully the wealth of dramatic creativeness that went into the
writing of *The Crucible*. Even if Miller did not succeed in drawing
his epic material completely together, he created a powerful drama
which overshadows current drama here or abroad. It may be sufficient
to congratulate ourselves on the presence of Arthur Miller in our
theatre. My major regret about this writer is that he is not enough of
a poet. I doubt that any post-Shakespearian dramatist could have
solved the problems inherent in Miller's material, but a true poet

could have transcended them. He could have placed the play beyond time and locality and carried us into the center of tragic vision. A more poetic playwright could also have economized on those parts of the plot that are necessarily merely transitional and supplementary and therefore are relatively flat.

Hysteria and Ideology in *The Crucible*

by *Richard Hayes*

It is altogether possible that Mr. Arthur Miller was prompted to the composition of his latest play by the malign politico-cultural pressures of our society, but whatever the impulse, it has issued in a drama of arresting polemic distinction.

The Crucible does not, I confess, seem to me a work of such potential tragic force as the playwright's earlier *Death of a Salesman*; it is the product of theatrical dexterity and a young man's moral passion, rather than of a fruitful and reverberating imagination. But it has, in a theatre of the small success and the tidy achievement, power, the passionate line—an urgent boldness which does not shrink from the implications of a large and formidable design.

With the Salem witchcraft trials of 1692 as a moral frame and point of departure, Mr. Miller has gone on to examine the permanent conditions of the climate of hysteria. The New England tragedy was for him, dramatically, a fortuitous choice because it is accessible to us imaginatively; as one of the few severely irrational eruptions American society has witnessed, it retains still its primitive power to compel the attention. And it exhibits, moreover, the several features of the classically hysterical situation: the strange moral alchemy by which the accused becomes inviolable; the disrepute which overtakes the testimony of simple intelligence; the insistence on public penance; the willingness to absolve if guilt is confessed.

It is *imaginative* terror Mr. Miller is here invoking: not the solid gallows and the rope appall him, but the closed and suffocating world of the fanatic, against which the intellect and will are powerless.

Excerpted from "Hysteria and Ideology in The Crucible" *[editor's title] by Richard Hayes. From* Commonweal *57 (February 1953), 498. Copyright © 1953 by* Commonweal. *Reprinted by permission of the publisher.*

It is a critical commonplace that the commitments of Mr. Miller's plays are ideological rather than personal—that he does not create a world so much in its simple humanity, or its perceptible reality, as in its intellectual alarms and excursions. *The Crucible* reinforces this tradition.

Despite the fact that he is often at his best in the "realist" vein, Mr. Miller, like any good heir of the thirties, is preoccupied with ideology. He has a richer personal sense of it than comparable writers, but the impulse remains unaltered. His characteristic theme is integrity, and its obverse, compromise. In earlier plays, Miller frequently brought to this subject a distressing note of stridency; one often felt that, really, the battle had long since been won, and that this continued obsession with it was an indication not of seriousness, but perhaps of some arrested moral development.

In *The Crucible*, however, he has stated his theme again with a wholly admirable concision and force. His central figure is John Proctor, another spokesman for rational feeling and the disinterested intelligence. Proctor is so patently the enemy of hysteria that his very existence is a challenge to the fanatic temperament, and he is consumed by its malice. What gives the situation a fresh vitality is Miller's really painful grasp of its ambiguities: the dilemma of a man, fallible, subject to pride, but forced to choose between the "negative good" of truth and morality, and the "positive good" of human life under any dispensation. Around this crisis of conscience, Mr. Miller has written an exhaustive, exacerbated scene—one of his most truly distinguished, and one which most hopefully displays the expanding delicacy of his moral imagination.

It is difficult, however, to feel that the political complexities inherent in *The Crucible* have been approached by Mr. Miller with any comparable sensitivity. He has, admittedly, disclaimed intent of contemporary reference in the play, choosing to see in it only the tragedy of another society. But it would be fatuous of Mr. Miller to pretend that our present cultural climate had not always a place in the foreground of his mind. Surely then, he can see that the Salem witch-hunts and our own virulent varieties are parallel only in their effects, not in their causes.

Dramatically, *The Crucible* maintains always that provocative interest and distinction one has come to associate with the work of this playwright. Mr. Miller has, on the whole, handled the Puritan idiom discreetly, despite the somewhat "official" taint of the weak prologue, and several unfortunate lapses into the contemporary. Mr. Miller *will* have his poetry, though; in *Death of a Salesman* he often resorted to a kind of bastard Whitman rhetoric, while *The Crucible*, especially in its hysterical imagery, owes an inordinate debt to the King James Bible. But language is handled here generally with considerable skill and sensibility.

Of the production at the Martin Beck, one can have very little criticism. Arthur Kennedy plays Proctor with all his assured style and intense virility, while Walter Hampden, Beatrice Straight and E. G. Marshall lend a grave and sober excellence to other figures in this Salem landscape. Mr. Jed Harris has directed boldly, with no shyness of scenes and curtains operatic in their intensity (and what a splendid opera might be made out of the Salem trials, incidentally). What *The Crucible* enriches and again asserts is the range, the variety and continuing interest of the American polemic tradition. . . .

A Problem Playwright

by Walter Kerr

Arthur Miller is a problem playwright, in both senses of the word. As a man of independent thought, he is profoundly, angrily concerned with the immediate issues of our society—with the irresponsible pressures which are being brought to bear on free men, with the self-seeking which blinds whole segments of our civilization to justice, with the evasions and dishonesties into which cowardly men are daily slipping. And to his fiery editorializing he brings shrewd theatrical gifts: He knows how to make a point plain, how to give it bite in the illustration, how to make its caustic and cauterizing language ring out on the stage.

He is also an artist groping toward something more poetic than simple, savage journalism. He has not only the professional crusader's zeal for humanity, but the imaginative writer's feeling for it —how it really behaves, how it moves about a room, how it looks in its foolish as well as in its noble attitudes—and in his best play, *Death of a Salesman,* he was able to rise above the sermon and touch the spirit of some simple people.

In *The Crucible,* which opened at the Martin Beck Thursday, he seems to me to be taking a step backward into mechanical parable, into the sort of play which lives not in the warmth of humbly observed human souls but in the ideological heat of polemic.

Make no mistake about it: There is fire in what Mr. Miller has to say, and there is a good bit of sting in his manner of saying it. He has, for convenience's sake, set his troubling narrative in the Salem of 1692. For reasons of their own, a quartet of exhibitionistic young women are hurling accusations of witchcraft at eminently respectable members of a well-meaning, but not entirely clear-headed, society.

On the basis of hearsay—"guilt by association with the devil" might be the phrase for it—a whole community of innocents are brought to trial and condemned to be hanged. As Mr. Miller pursues his very clear contemporary parallel, there are all sorts of relevant thrusts: The folk who do the final damage are not the lunatic fringe but the gullible pillars of society; the courts bog down into travesty in order to comply with the popular mood; slander becomes the weapon of opportunists ("Is the accuser always holy now?"); freedom is possible at the price of naming one's associates in crime; even the upright man is eventually tormented into going along with the mob to secure his own way of life, his own family.

Much of this—not all—is an accurate reading of our own turbulent age, and there are many times at the Martin Beck when one's intellectual sympathies go out to Mr. Miller and to his apt symbols anguishing on the stage. But it is the intellect which goes out, not the heart.

For Salem, and the people who live, love, fear and die in it, are really only conveniences to Mr. Miller, props to his thesis. He does not make them interesting in and for themselves, and you wind up analyzing them, checking their dilemmas against the latest headlines, rather than losing yourself in any rounded, deeply rewarding personalities. You stand back and think; you don't really share very much. . . .

PART THREE

Interpretations

A "Social Play"

by Leonard Moss

After *Focus, All My Sons,* and *Death of a Salesman,* many play-goers decided that Arthur Miller was a topical dramatist who dealt with injustices in American society such as anti-Semitism and capitalistic exploitation of the "common man." *The Crucible* confirmed their interpretation. This work, they assumed, addressed itself to that controversial subject of the early 1950's, Senator Joseph McCarthy's investigations of Communist subversion in the United States. Miller had apparently camouflaged his condemnation of those proceedings with the tale of an equally notorious witch-hunt conducted at Salem in 1692. The analogy seemed clear enough even though the setting of the play was a Massachusetts colony; the government, a Puritan "theocracy"; the prosecutor, Deputy Governor Danforth; and the subversives, Satan's agents disguised as ordinary townsfolk.

Miller did not deny the obvious contemporary relevance, but insisted that he was concerned with a problem larger than the current investigations. Senator McCarthy's activities, "a kind of personification of [moral] disintegration," [1] symbolized a dehumanizing influence that might occur in any period. His subject was mass hysteria: He wished to show how it could be fomented by self-appointed (and self-seeking) saviors; what its social and psychological consequences

---

"A 'Social Play'" [*editor's title*]. *From the chapter "Four 'Social Plays'" in Leonard Moss,* Arthur Miller *(New York: Twayne Publishers, Inc., 1967), pp. 59–66. Copyright © 1967 by Twayne Publishers, Inc. Reprinted by permission of the publishers.*
1. Miller's phrase in Henry Brandon, "The State of the Theatre," *Harper's,* 221 (November 1960), 66.

might be; and how it must be averted. "It was not only the rise of 'McCarthyism' that moved me, but something which seemed much more weird and mysterious. It was the fact that a political, objective, knowledgeable campaign from the far Right was capable of creating not only a terror, but a new subjective reality, a veritable mystique which was gradually assuming even a holy resonance. . . . The terror in these people was being knowingly planned and consciously engineered, and yet all they knew was terror" (*Collected Plays*, pp. 39–40). *The Crucible* may well be called a "social play," since it analyzes a public phenomenon with historical precedent and current actuality. But it focuses on the "subjective reality" of that phenomenon; it cannot be judged merely on the literal accuracy or political aptness of its topical allusions.

Miller explains the social and religious causes of the Puritan madness in a long commentary accompanying the play. Not everyone who contributed to that madness, he admits, was villainous. Some officials, like Danforth, Reverend Hale, and Judge Hathorne, committed the gravest wrongs in the name of the public welfare, as they conceived it. Salem was governed by "a combine of state and religious power whose function was to keep the community together, and to prevent any kind of disunity that might open it to destruction by material or ideological enemies." Any impatience with this power was curbed by harsh restrictive measures. The chief enemy to be exorcised was Satan; in formulating political policy, state authorities were able to enlist the Puritan's belief in the supernatural origin of good and evil. Miller's conclusion in this respect clearly refers to the analogous contemporary situation: "The necessity of the Devil may become evident as a weapon, a weapon designed and used time and time again in every age to whip men into a surrender to a particular church or church-state. . . . A political policy is equated with moral right, and opposition to it with diabolical malevolence."

Greater harm, however, was done for personal than for political reasons. "Long-held hatreds of neighbors could now be openly expressed, and vengeance taken. . . . Land-lust . . . could now be elevated to the arena of morality." These egoistic motives are illustrated by minor details in the play: the quarrel between Putnam and Proctor over lumber, Reverend Parris's preoccupation with firewood and candleholders, and Giles's propensities for litigation. Selfish motives are also illustrated in the major incidents that magnify excitement prior to the explosion of hysteria; Miller sees bewitchment as a mental state that can be deliberately induced by unscrupulous individuals.

The method used by malicious figures like Abigail and the Putnams to gain control over the frightened, the gullible, and the weakwilled is indeed diabolical. They first completely demoralize their victim, then subtly implant in him the terms of a confession that will release him from suspicion and at the same time achieve their own devious ends. When *The Crucible* begins, the reported discovery of the girls' dancing has already instilled fear of demonic infiltration in the community. Reverend Parris, his daughter suspected of devilworship, eagerly grasps at suggestions carefully insinuated by the Putnams, a couple bearing "many grievances." Mrs. Putnam thoroughly shakes the minister with her "vicious certainty" that his daughter Betty has commerced with the Devil, after which Putnam cunningly prescribes a plan to divert public notice: "You are not undone! Let you take hold here. Wait for no one to charge you— declare it yourself. You have discovered witchcraft." The terrified girl, as well as her intimidated father, seizes upon the words of this clever husband-wife team; overhearing Mrs. Putnam ask, "How high did she fly, how high?" Betty cries, "I'll fly to Mama. Let me fly!" In this way, knaves gain control of fools, brush aside the sane counsels of those who try to exert a calming influence, and initiate Salem's passion.

Reverend Hale, a scholarly expert on deviltry, signals the next stage in the growth of panic. Motivated by a "tasty love of intellectual pursuit" (author's note), he is more sincere than the Putnams, but he mercilessly continues the attack on poor whimpering Betty by driving at the theme introduced earlier by Mrs. Putnam (and taken up later by Abigail, the prime instigator of the witch hunt): "Does someone afflict you, child? . . . Perhaps some bird invisible to others comes to you. . . . Is there some figure bids you fly?" When the chorus of interrogators—Hale, the Putnams, Abigail, and Parris—turns from Betty to Tituba, the impressionable Negro slave is so terrified that she eagerly reaches for the escape offered her by

Hale and Putnam—a confession of complicity with the Devil ("We will protect you. . . . And we will bless you, Tituba"). The manner in which they elicit specific responses through suggestion may be observed in this exchange:

> *Hale.* When the Devil comes to you does he ever come—with another
> person? . . .
> *Putnam.* Sarah Good? Did you ever see Sarah Good with him? Or
> Osburn? . . .
> *Tituba.* And then he come one stormy night to me, and he say, "Look!
> I have *white* people belong to me." And I look—and there was
> Goody Good. . . . Aye, sir, and Goody Osburn.

Abigail cleverly augments the uproar after Tituba's admission by adding her own; this act induces frenzy in the other girls and accelerates the chain reaction of accusation and confession.

These incidents, Miller notes, may be considered a kind of introduction or "overture" to the trial.[2] Following a fairly long expository interval during which Abigail brings about the imprisonment of her rival, Elizabeth Proctor, the deliberate implantation of irrational notions in susceptible minds continues in the climactic episode. Several conventional narrative devices prepare the stage. At the beginning of Act Three, two unseen characters are heard in conversation—the offstage-actor technique invented by Aeschylus. Then there is the plot formula based on an unjust trial of a just man, with a heated debate on salvation and damnation. The trial at first involves traditional courtroom theatrics—fierce charges and countercharges by the participants, shouted objections and periodic clamor from the "townspeople"—but Miller presently moves the hearing into a "vestry room" to create a more intimate stage setting. Another venerable plot convention, the fatal exposure of a lie, appears twice: once, when the court disproves Mary Warren's claim to be able to "pretend" fainting; again, when Governor Danforth discredits the veracity of John Proctor, the protagonist. In the second instance, as in *All My Sons,* a woman inadvertently betrays her husband, although here the basic device has been varied: Proctor is discredited,

2. Miller, quoted in Henry Hewes, "Broadway Postscript,' *Saturday Review,* 36 (January 31, 1953), 24.

ironically, because the lie is *believed* (Elizabeth affirms his marital fidelity), while the truth (that Abigail, the adulteress, wishes to supplant Elizabeth) is disbelieved.

With Proctor's case demolished, Abigail vigorously resumes her brilliant impersonation of a soul possessed. Pushed beyond the bounds of sanity by Abigail's performance, by the spectacular gyrations of her friends, and by that effective convincer, "confess yourself or you will hang," Mary Warren, who might have testified to Abigail's "private vengeance" against Elizabeth, breaks down—another victim of induced hysteria. Her ecstatic transports intensify the wildly melodramatic climax (the stage directions call for "gigantic screams" from the girls as they stare at an imaginary "bird"), and Proctor histrionically protests the triumph of unreason: "You are pulling Heaven down and raising up a whore!"

In constructing this "interior mechanism of confession and forgiveness" (*Collected Plays*, p. 40), Miller places special emphasis on the insidious role played by certain individuals. It would be an oversimplification, however, to say that he conceives the conflict as one between innocent and wicked figures. The characters in *The Crucible* may better be described as either maturing or ethically fixed personalities—a distinction relevant to Lawrence Newman and Carlson in *Focus,* Chris and Joe Keller in *All My Sons,* Biff and Willy Loman in *Death of a Salesman.* Whether self-righteous, vindictive, or merely escapist, those who share the responsibility for bringing on the disaster are mentally static or unstable, however dynamic they might be in action. They continue to enforce blindly, to manipulate ruthlessly, or to follow fearfully sanctified standards of conduct even when to do so becomes absurd and destructive.

Miller underlines their inflexibility by characterizing them in a mechanical fashion. Although Abigail has a few passionate lines as a jealous lover, she functions primarily as a catalyst in the intimidation–confession process. Others fall into more stereotyped patterns— Parris, the ranting paranoiac; Mary Warren and her friends, the malleable children; Tituba, the frightened, somewhat comic darky; Danforth, the uncompromising but misguided judge. Some of the wholly admirable figures are also stock types, like Giles Corey (the gruff, honest farmer) and Rebecca Nurse (the calm, comforting, wise old matriarch). For the reader, Miller's notes heighten the impres-

sion of static characterization when they anticipate a character's first
lines, as in these instances:

AUTHOR'S NOTE. [Parris] believed he was being persecuted wherever he
went, despite his best efforts to win people and God to his side.

Parris. I do not fathom it, why am I persecuted here? I cannot offer one
proposition but there be a howling riot of argument. I have often
wondered if the Devil be in it somewhere; I cannot understand you
people otherwise.

AUTHOR'S NOTE. Danforth is a grave man in his sixties, of some humor
and sophistication that does not, however, interfere with an exact
loyalty to his position and his cause.

Danforth. While I speak God's law, I will not crack its voice with whimpering. If retaliation is your fear, know this—I should hang ten
thousand that dared to rise against the law, and an ocean of salt tears
could not melt the resolution of the statutes.

In opposition to these predetermined behavior patterns, three
characters—deficient at first in "charity" and immersed in self-
concern—eventually make humane, courageous, and rational adjustments to the formidable challenges confronting them. The moral
growth of Reverend Hale and the Proctors contrasts on one hand
with the rigidity of Abigail, Hathorne, and Danforth, and on the
other with the instability of Tituba, Parris, and the girls. Reverend
Hale seems unpromising as a candidate for change. A note intro-
duces him as a stock figure—a smug intellectual with "the pride of
the specialist whose unique knowledge has at last been publicly
called for." His words bear out this description: "Here is all the invisible world, caught, defined, and calculated," he lectures. "In these
books the Devil stands stripped of all his brute disguises." But the
"deeply honest" minister, sickened at last by the gross injustice he
has abetted, later denounces the judges. Elizabeth too arrives at
greater understanding. Initially adamant in her condemnation of
her husband's single adulterous act ("You forget nothin' and forgive
nothin'," Proctor complains; "learn charity, woman"), she acquires
a tolerance for human fallibility and an appreciation for human
goodness during her trial and imprisonment.

John Proctor does not advance, like Elizabeth and Hale, from
vanity to charity. He progresses in a different direction—from shame

to renewed assurance. For a time his humility as an adulterer disposes him to accept the greater humiliation of confessing to witchcraft; since he has already blackened his "good name" by succumbing to and then publicly admitting lechery, he is tempted to save at least his life. Indignation, however, compels him to salvage self-respect: "How may I live without my name? . . . Show honor now, show a stony heart and sink them with it." With exalted victory-in-defeat rhetoric he proclaims his rediscovery of what he thought had been lost—a "sense of personal inviolability. . . . That's what Proctor means near the end of the play when he talks of his 'name.' He is really speaking about his identity, which he cannot surrender." [3]

The Crucible, then, explores two contrary processes in the context of a given social order—the generation of hysteria and the achievement of moral honesty. How successfully are the two processes integrated? The first three acts are very well structured. Through an expository method Miller favored in earlier plays—delayed revelation of past sins—he reveals, in retrospect, that the central psychosocial issue of witchcraft arose from the private issue involving Abigail, John, and Elizabeth Proctor—a Puritanical variant of the eternal triangle. Among the few covert early allusions to the seduction are Parris's remark that Elizabeth "comes so rarely to the church this year for she will not sit so close to something soiled [Abigail]," and Betty's comment to Abigail, "You drank a charm to kill Goody Proctor!" Abigail's passion for Proctor, which moves her to attack Elizabeth through the witch-hunt, provides the chief causal link between the private and public issues even though it remains of secondary dramatic importance. The second act, a transitional interlude bridging the introductory and climactic episodes, builds suspense and develops the two subjects preparatory to their simultaneous resolution in the trial scene. In the third act, Proctor and Hale cannot turn aside the forces maneuvered by Abigail, and the action ascends to its shrill emotional peak.

During this well-balanced ascent toward insanity, Proctor's personal difficulties are subordinate to Salem's ordeal. The conclusion abruptly reverses that relationship in a last-act shift of interest similar to, though not so disruptive as, the shift in *All My Sons*. Without warning, Miller's exhibition of devil-possession ceases. Having

3. Miller, quoted in Hewes, p. 25.

sparked Salem's "fire," Abigail disappears; "the legend has it that Abigail turned up later as a prostitute in Boston," a footnote explains. Moreover, it seems that even as "terror" was spreading unchecked in Salem, the condemnations were being called into question elsewhere in the area. The authority of the prosecutors has suddenly come to depend upon confession by those victims recently condemned, so that continued defiance by a highly regarded citizen like John Proctor will cure the town's fever. If Abigail's desire to supplant Elizabeth was the prime excitant of the madness, Proctor's desire to preserve his "name" becomes the prime depressant. When the protagonist realizes he cannot betray himself and his friends with a false confession, he at once completes his progression toward integrity and diverts Salem from its movement toward chaos.

The first consequence offers a consistent and positive, if unpleasant, denouement: Facing execution in an irrational society, a man asserts his will to judge his own honesty and to oppose injustice. The second consequence, however, does not logically follow from the preceding action. Only some misgivings voiced by Parris and Hale support the premise that *Proctor's* salvation will ensure *Salem's* salvation. "Andover have thrown out the court, they say, and will have no part of witchcraft," Parris reports. "There be a faction here, feeding on that news, and I tell you true, sir, I fear there will be riot here." He protests to the judges that "it were another sort that hanged till now. . . . These people have great weight yet in the town." Hale alerts the governor to "orphans wandering from house to house; abandoned cattle bellow on the highroads, the stink of rotting crops hangs everywhere, and no man knows when the harlots' cry will end his life—and you wonder yet if rebellion's spoke?" This reportorial narration cannot carry the heavy causal burden placed upon it. Nor can Proctor's last brave speeches, inspiring as they sound, account for the fact that after his hanging (Miller adds in a postscript) "the power of theocracy in Massachusetts was broken." How does Proctor's courage interrupt the "interior mechanism of confession and forgiveness"? What psychological impact does self-sacrifice have upon those who have triggered and those who have been crushed by that mechanism? The notion implied in the conclusion, that society may be redeemed by its maturest citizens, is an affirmative one. But this optimistic expectation, while intellectually gratifying, does not jibe with the traumatic agitation of the climax or with the quiet sorrow at the close.[4]

4. Miller may have been betrayed by following his probable source too closely. Upham's *Salem Witchcraft*, otherwise extremely comprehensive, flags at this point also: "A sudden collapse took place in the machinery, and [the court] met no more. . . . The curtain fell unexpectedly and the tragedy ended. It is not known precisely what caused this sudden change. . . . It has generally been attributed to the fact that the girls became over-confident and struck too high" (Ungar edition, II, 344).

Dramatic Technique in *The Crucible*

by Edward Murray

. . . The main characters in *Crucible*, contrary to some critical reports, are far from flat. John Proctor is described as a "farmer in his middle thirties," "powerful of body." In his first scene, John reveals himself as a man with a strong personality: "Abigail has stood as though on tiptoe, absorbing his presence, wide-eyed," while the other girl is "strangely titillated." That Abigail is willing to murder in order to possess John invests this farmer with a sense of importance. That John lusted with the girl in the past—against the law of God and Salem—reveals a certain daring in the man. That John has the will power to resist Abigail now, even while part of him still desires her, shows determination. Repeatedly, John displays his dislike of authoritarianism.

In Act Two, John makes a determined effort to please Elizabeth. He kisses her perfunctorily; he lies in saying that her cooking is well-seasoned (perhaps a kind of irony on the lack of spice in Elizabeth?). John seems motivated by guilt feelings in this scene. When Elizabeth urges him to go to court and expose Abigail, he is afraid that his relations with the girl will be brought to light. The question of whether the court will believe him would seem of secondary importance. The cardinal point is that John must struggle against his own fear. Miller attempts to integrate the "personal" and the "social" in a number of ways. "I cannot speak but I am doubted," says John, ". . . as though I come into a court when I come into this house!" Although John lies to Elizabeth about being alone with Abigail in Parris's house, he persists in defending his honesty.

John continues to struggle, throughout Act Three, against both his inner contradictions and his outer antagonists. He reveals his resourcefulness in securing a deposition. He shows his persistence in extracting a confession from Mary. When the charge against Elizabeth is suspended, John does not falter—he concentrates his attack on the court for the sake of others. And when Abigail seems to be winning the struggle, John makes public confession of his "lechery."

In Act Four, John "is another man, bearded, filthy, his eyes misty as though webs had overgrown them." The physical transformation signals an inner change in John. "I have been thinking," he tells Elizabeth, "I would confess to them." After a few months in jail contemplating his death, a change of appearance and attitude on John's part is credible. John defends himself by saying: "Spite only keeps me silent"; "I want my life." However, John has not overcome his inner conflict; he hesitates to implicate others; he balks at signing the confession. Gradually, John moves to a position of final defiance of the court: "I have three children—how may I teach them to walk like men . . . and I sold my friends?"

The foregoing shows clearly that John is rich in traits; that there is continuous development of his character; and that there is adequate preparation for his revelation in the last act.

No critic, as far as I know, has questioned John Proctor's status as a "tragic hero." The controversy over the "common man" versus the "traditional hero" (usually Aristotelian), occasioned by the fate of Willy Loman, is absent from discussions of *Crucible*. Miller would seem to have provided Proctor with all the heroic attributes dear to the heart of "traditionalists." Miller himself says: "In *The Crucible* . . . the characters were special people who could give voice to the things that were inside them. . . . These people knew what was happening to them" (*Theatre Arts*, October 1953). Whether this increase in articulateness makes *Crucible* a more powerful dramatic piece than *Death of a Salesman* is arguable.

Dialogue, it should be noted, fails to illuminate John's past. Is this lack of background a serious failing in *Crucible*? In *All My Sons*, lack of adequate character exposition impaired credibility; in *Salesman*, the revelation of Willy's past had a direct bearing on the present line of development. In *Crucible*, however, the past would not seem to be pertinent. Each play should be approached on its own merits. *Crucible* focuses on a specific situation, and the reader possesses all the necessary facts for believing in that situation. Nor should one conclude that, since John's final speeches sound too theatrical, the language in the play is not adequate. The various summaries presented in this chapter should indicate that preparation, especially foreshadowing of character development, is expertly handled. Miller, in a very subtle manner, uses key words to knit together the texture of action and theme. Note, for example, the recurrent use of the word "soft." In Act One, John tells Abigail: "Abby, I may think of you *softly* from time to time . . ." (italics mine); in Act Two, Hale tells John: "there is a *softness* in your record, sir, a *softness*" (italics mine). Dialogue, moreover, suggests that behind John's denunciation of Parris lies a guilty conscience. Hale says that John has missed church services a good deal in the past seventeen months; since Abigail has been removed from Proctor's house for the past seven months, the inference is that the real reason for John's backsliding has not been expressed.

Miller is even more sparing than usual in his physical description of Elizabeth; that is, not one word is uttered about her appearance. Nor, as was the case with John, is anything conveyed about her background. Nevertheless, Elizabeth has many traits and she grows throughout the play. She is sensitive: "It hurt my heart to strip her, poor rabbit"; here, of course, Elizabeth is a foil to the murderous Abigail. Elizabeth betrays a weakness in asserting herself against Mary Warren, a weakness which John brands a "fault." She is also proud, slow to forgive, and suspicious. Frequently, Elizabeth—who is "cold"—fails in charity. But she will lie for a loved one, and, since she learns humility, she is capable of change. Elizabeth's dominant motive is her yearning for John's undivided love. In Act Two, for instance, behind Elizabeth's self-righteous and intolerant posture, there is love for John. She proves this love in Act Three when she lies to save John's life. Elizabeth continues to grow in the last act. . . .

Abigail is much less complex and interesting than either John or Elizabeth. She is described as "seventeen . . . a strikingly beautiful girl, an orphan, with an endless capacity for dissembling." Dialogue fails to disclose anything about Abigail's past. In the course of the play, however, she reveals several traits: she is supersensitive, sexually passionate, and mentally alert; she is commanding and vain;

she is a thief; and throughout the play, she makes painfully evident that she is capable of murder. Abigail's dominant motive is to destroy Elizabeth and sleep with John. Abigail remains in character; but she does not grow.

The minor characters, with the exception of Hale, are flat and static. There is a question of Miller's economy here, and Miller himself was not unaware of the problem. In *All My Sons,* Miller seemed to have employed more characters than he needed for the furtherance of either action or theme. In *The Crucible,* in spite of the fact that there are at least twenty-one characters, the problem does not seem acute, for, as was pointed out in the discussion of structure, Miller managed to keep the developing action in thematic focus. If the numerous characters, such as Marshall Herrick or Ezekiel Cheever, contribute very little, if anything, to action or theme, it is also true that they do nothing to impede or becloud action and theme. Some readers might find many of these secondary figures mere "scenery"; whether Miller might have profitably eliminated them entirely is an interesting, but hardly a burning, technical question. . . .

Danforth, it is important to remember, is motivated by the fact that he is an orthodox Puritan who fully believes in the existence of evil spirits. As the symbol of authority, Danforth assumes exact knowledge of "God's law," and, taking a rigid stance on the letter of that law, he pursues the logic of what he conceives the facts to be to their inevitable end. Danforth's mind, the mind of a lawyer, makes sharp, rational distinctions: For him, a principle is sacred, and he would not hesitate, since he sees his way clearly, to sacrifice all human life for a single principle. Like many God-surrogates, Danforth seems to be a proud man; but behind his stiff posture there now and then lurks the fear, never wholly embraced or articulated, that he might be in serious error. After Danforth has sentenced nearly one hundred men and women to be hanged, he has a *personal* stake in the justice of the trials; he is almost coerced into assuming an "either-or" view of good and evil, for to admit the unknowable, the ambiguous, the irrational, into experience would be to expose "God" [read Danforth and Salem law] to the confusion and uncertainty of a world suddenly turned upside down by inexplicable events.

Hale might be considered as a foil to Danforth. He begins as fully confident of his moral position as the Deputy-Governor, for in his books, Hale has evil neatly "caught, defined, and calculated." Life, however, refutes the books; and Hale, more sensitive than Danforth, more comprehending, permits doubt to enter, like a corrosive chemical, into his soul. As a result, Hale no longer is convinced that he is privy to the decrees of the most high; on the contrary, asserting that God's will is often in darkness, he assumes the radical ambiguity of moral questions. Where Danforth declares that he would "hang ten thousand that dared to rise against the law," Hale avers: "Life is God's most precious gift; no principle . . . may justify the taking of it."

Rebecca Nurse resembles the very man who condemns her to be hanged. Like Danforth, she would not sacrifice a principle even if it should cost her her life. Like Danforth, she appears to have no sense of guilt; she tells John: "Let you fear nothing! Another judgment waits us all!" Like Danforth, Rebecca sees little of life's complexity (are there no "real-life" counterparts to Danforth and Rebecca?); she is merely "astonished" at John's lie to save his life.

Giles Corey's position on the thematic spectrum suggests a stance somewhere between the extremes of "nobility" (represented by those who take morals seriously) and "ignobility" (Parris, say, or the Putnams). Although Giles fights against the evil of the trials, he dies— not for the sake of an abstract principle of right—but in such a way as to insure that his property will go to his sons.

Elizabeth Proctor is more complex than Danforth, Hale, Giles, and Rebecca. Elizabeth, like Hale, is willing to sacrifice an abstraction when it seems, to her, expedient to do so; but, unlike Hale, she does not "rationalize" her argument; "subjective," not "objective" arguments dictate her actions. In Act Two, Elizabeth sacrifices logic to her pride; she tells Hale that she believes in the Gospels (and the Gospels affirm the existence of witches); but she adds that if Hale thinks that she could "do only good work in the world, and yet be secretly bound to Satan, then I must tell you, sir, I do not believe it." In Act Three, Elizabeth sacrifices a principle to save her husband's life; her motive here is not pride, as it was above, but love. In Act Four, she refuses to answer John's question whether she would lie to save her own life; John believes that she would not lie. On the basis of her record, how can John—or the reader—be certain? Elizabeth says she wants John alive—which scarcely allows John much choice in the matter. No longer self-righteous, Elizabeth stresses her own frailty; repeatedly she says: "I cannot judge you, John"; and she adds: "Whatever you will do, it is a good man does it." This is important. Elizabeth seems to be saying that a man may lie and be "good"—or, equally, a man may refuse to lie and be "good." How can this be "true"? It would seem idle to argue the matter philosophically or semantically; for instance, one might say that "good" is a vague term, or that Elizabeth means that John has not confessed until now, and regardless of what he does later, that (as Elizabeth tells John) "speak goodness in you." However, it would seem more rewarding, for the critic if not the philosopher, to ask: What has Elizabeth revealed about herself that permits her to hold such a belief? Early in Act Four, when Hale suggests that Elizabeth persuade John to lie in order to save himself, she says: "I think that be the Devil's argument"; but when faced by John, she says, in effect, that a man might use the "Devil's argument" and still be a "good" man. Elizabeth is not inconsistent here; we have seen that she has previously sacrificed principle for personal ends; we have also seen that she has reached a stage in her growth toward humility when she is, at least for the moment, more concerned with the "beam in her own eye."

John Proctor's response to events is, of course, the most complicated one in the play; moreover, his role as protagonist would appear to lend his position more validity than that of the other characters. Since John's development has been traced above, little need be added here. It is worth stressing, however, that John thought he was "good" in Act Two; but as it developed, John was self-deceived—in his heart, he still lusted after Abigail. At the end of the play, John again believes in his "goodness"; but Hale, in effect, says that John is once again self-deceived: "It is pride, it is vanity."

. . . *The Crucible* would not seem to be the simple, didactic, polemical play that most critics, including Miller himself perhaps, would have us believe. Although the characters, with the exception of John, Elizabeth, and possibly Hale, are constructed along relatively simple lines, the multiple points of view are complex and well-orchestrated. . . .

The play is complex because John *is* a "good" man; so is Hale; so is Giles; Elizabeth and Rebecca are "good" too—for only "good" people do battle with evil. Even Danforth is not black—given his cast of mind and the times, one can, at least, understand his position (those who call him "wholly guilty" would seem to be doing the play an injustice through oversimplification). . . .

Granting, it might be objected, that *Crucible* contains more variety than is usually allowed for it, is it not true that it remains a bit too simple? For some readers, the neatness of the thematic spectrum is perhaps an argument against the play's complexity, and for those who demand shading, not among multiple points of view but in each individual character, Miller's play is unsatisfactory. The same readers may also feel that Proctor's infidelity is not enough of a complication, that it is too flimsy a foundation on which to erect the structure of *Crucible*. The crucial question, however, is: Does Miller succeed in fusing the "personal" and the "social"? A close reading of the play would suggest that he does. A flaw in Proctor's marriage allows the trials to materialize; no act—even the most intimate of sexual relations—would seem isolated from the "social." Elizabeth admits to being "cold"; but it is not due to being "puritanical," as some critics would have it, or to "lack of love"; she says (as I have quoted previously): "John, I counted myself so plain, so poorly made, no honest love could come to me! . . . I never knew how I should say my love." John asks: "Is the accuser always holy now?" This has both a "personal" and a "social" reference; "personal" because Elizabeth accuses John of evil and she is not "holy" (although she admits her faults later), while John himself learns that he is not as "holy" as he had thought; "social" because, to take but one instance, Abigail and the girls are not "holy" but they accuse others. This much is fairly obvious. . . . Is it necessary that the guilt be of a single kind? Is it not possible—indeed probable—that various kinds of guilt may come to focus upon a single "social" situation? Of course, Elizabeth admits to keeping a "cold house"; and Salem is a "cold" community; and the activity of the girls in the woods suggests sexual repression—but this is far from being the entire explanation of events. And, as Miller *dramatizes* his material, guilt is not the sole motive for the trials. Nor would it seem either necessary or desirable that it should be in order to link the "personal" to the "social." Some critics want a single explanation for the "enemy"; but certainly the interest of the play, for a mature reader, is that the "enemy" assumes many shapes and refuses to be reduced to a single motivation. Mrs. Putnam is filled with hate because she lost seven babies at birth; Mr. Putnam wants land; Parris wants to protect his job; Tituba wants to save her neck; Abigail wants John—and so it goes. If it be objected that few of these characters seem genuinely convinced of witchcraft, that would seem to be more of an historical than an aesthetic question. Miller, it must be owned, exposed himself to such criticism by identifying his play with a specific period. It is certainly arguable whether we get, as Miller says we do, the "essential nature" of the Salem trials; but no matter—what we do get is an extremely effective drama. . . .

The Devil in Salem

by Dennis Welland

. . . To begin with, it is of interest as an historical play, by which
I mean something more than a mere costume-drama. Miller provides a note on its historical accuracy which indicates the care he
has taken over it, and reference to Marion Starkey's account or to
the primary sources will quickly substantiate this. . . . To document this would be tedious: sufficient, perhaps, to mention as an
example the book written in 1697 by John Hale: *A Modest Inquiry
into the Nature of Witchcraft.*[1] There is an obvious identity between Miller's character in *The Crucible* and the man whose ambi-
valent attitude to the whole proceedings may be seen from the following extracts:

> I observed in the prosecution of these affairs, that there was in the
> Justices, Judges and others concerned, a conscientious endeavour to
> do the thing that was right.

Nevertheless, he is not easy in his own conscience, though what he
questions is legal procedure rather than witchcraft itself:

> We may hence see ground to fear that there hath been a great deal
> of innocent blood shed in the Christian World, by proceeding upon
> unsafe principles, in condemning persons for Malefick Witchcraft.

There is a similar reservation in his recognition of the need for resti-
tution to some (not, apparently, to all) of the victims:

Excerpted from "The Devil in Salem." From Dennis Welland, Arthur Miller
*(Oliver and Boyd, Edinburgh, 1961), pp. 74–91. Copyright © 1961 by Oliver and
Boyd, Edinburgh. Reprinted by permission of the publisher.*
   1. Published posthumously in Boston, 1702. Reprinted in *Narratives of the
Witchcraft Cases*, ed. G. L. Burr (New York, 1914). The quotations given are
from this reprint, pp. 415, 425, 427, 431.

I would humbly propose whether it be not expedient, that some what more should be publickly done than yet hath, for clearing the good name and reputation of some that have suffered upon this account.

Hale is prepared to admit that he and his colleagues may have made mistakes in an excess of zeal; he is still convinced that witchcraft may exist and that vigilance must be maintained:

Seeing we have been too hard against supposed Malefick Witchcraft, let us take heed we do not on the contrary become too favourable to divining Witchcraft [*sc.* fortune-telling].

The note of uncertainty, of suspended judgment, that these quotations reveal is very close to the keynote of this play, which I find in the constant recurrence, on the lips of many different characters, of the phrase "I think." Much of the play could be summarised in Yeats's lines:

The best lack all conviction, while the worst
Are full of passionate intensity.

It is not so much a story of two ideologies in conflict as a story of conscientious endeavour in an uncertain world. This emerges with particular force and clarity in Act II, in, for example, such exchanges as this, in which Elizabeth Proctor tells her husband what she has heard from Mary Warren:

Elizabeth. The Deputy Governor promise hangin' if they'll not confess, John. The town's gone wild, I think. She speak of Abigail, and I thought she were a saint, to hear her. . . .
Proctor. Oh, it is a black mischief.
Elizabeth. I think you must go to Salem, John. I think so. You must tell them it is a fraud.

Joe Keller had asked in vain for guidance: No one could give it to him. Willy Loman's bewilderment at Charley, who had never told his son what to do, is the bewilderment of the man who has confidently inculcated in his own sons a complete set of values that have turned out to be wrong (just as Ben's advice to Biff, "Never fight fair with a stranger, boy," is, in its context, implicitly criticised). In *The Crucible* the wiser characters do not presume to dictate anyone's duty to him, for that would be asking him to hand over his conscience. Moreover, they themselves are too perplexed by the con-

flicting implications of the issues to be dogmatic. Elizabeth's quietly
delivered suggestions here are the thoughts of a worried but honest
mind spoken aloud for her husband's benefit, and he replies in the
same key: "I'll think on it. . . . I think it is not easy to prove she's
fraud, and the town gone so silly." Far from indicating a limited
vocabulary, either of character or author, the repetition of this formula "I think" is in fact a very skilfully managed way of suggesting
the scruples, the misgivings, and the conscientious earnestness which
are all that these people can bring against the diabolic impetus of
the witch-hunt. It is significant that Miller chose to dramatise the
story of John Proctor, the plain farmer, rather than the equally well-
documented story of George Burrough, the minister, who was also
accused of witchcraft and hanged for it. Miller's invention of Proctor's earlier adultery with Abigail is not the outcome of a mercenary
desire to add a spice of sensationalism to the play. It is a similar
insistence on the human vulnerability of a man who is not a saint,
not even an ordained minister fortified by a theological training, but
just a decent man trying to understand and to translate into action
the dictates of his conscience, trying to do, not what he *feels,* but
what he *thinks,* is right. . . .

In American literature, probably more than in any other, there
have always been influences at work to minimise the fact of evil. At
the extreme there is the Emersonian Transcendentalism optimis-
tically asserting that "Good is positive. Evil is merely privative, not
absolute: it is like cold, which is the privation of heat," and "There
is no pure lie, no pure malignity in nature. The entertainment of
the proposition of depravity is the last profligacy and profanation." [2]
The Declaration of Independence may be said to have made evil an
un-American activity, and although the buoyancy that American
literature acquires from this heritage of optimism is often invigo-
rating, yet it can be a limitation. Its writers have generally been
quicker to recognise evils than to recognise evil. Part of the superiority of Melville and James over Hawthorne lies in their ability to
conceive of evil where he thinks only in terms of sin, and Faulkner's
superiority over many of his contemporaries is in part attributable

  2. These quotations come respectively from "The Divinity School Address"
and the essay "New England Reformers."

to his awareness of evil where they see psychological maladjustment and environmental deprivation.

It is salutary, then, to find Miller enunciating this general belief in the need for literature to recognise evil, but it is a little disconcerting to find it in this specific context. The dedication to evil, of which he speaks, "not mistaking it for good, but *knowing it as evil* [my italics] and loving it as evil," may perhaps be imputed in this play—and we may disregard the sources in this discussion—to those characters who deliberately and cynically give false evidence, or incite others to do so, for their own personal gain or gratification. This means Thomas Putnam, with his greed for land, and Abigail, with her lust for Proctor. Putnam, however, is only a minor character, and Miller himself (as I shall shortly indicate) seems in two minds about the extent to which Abigail is evil or merely deluded. Evil can with much less certainty be imputed to the judges, who, hard and cruel as they may have been by our standards, and even culpably credulous, were trying, both in history and in the play, to judge in the light of evidence of an unprecedented nature. To make them more evil would be to destroy by distortion one of the virtues of the play in its present form. The very considerable dramatic power of *The Crucible* derives from its revelation of a mounting tide of evil gaining, in an entire society, an ascendancy quite disproportionate to the evil of any individual member of that society. What is so horrifying is to watch the testimony of honest men bouncing like an india-rubber ball off the high wall of disbelief that other men have built around themselves, not from ingrained evil, but from overzealousness and a purblind confidence in their own judgment. What meaning has proof when men will believe only what they want to believe, and will interpret evidence only in the light of their own prejudice? To watch *The Crucible* is to be overwhelmed by the simple impotence of honest common sense against fanaticism that is getting out of control, and to be painfully reminded that there are situations in which sheer goodness ("mere unaided virtue," in Melville's phrase about Starbuck) is just not enough to counter such deviousness.

. . . The real moral of the play is the very Shavian one that in the life of a society, evil is occasioned less by deliberate villainy than by the abnegation of personal responsibility. That is why Elizabeth quietly rejects as "the Devil's argument" Hale's impassioned plea:

> Beware, Goody Proctor—cleave to no faith when faith brings blood. It is a mistaken law that leads you to sacrifice. Life, woman, life is God's most precious gift; no principle, however glorious, may justify the taking of it.

Elizabeth, like St. Joan, has learnt through suffering that "God's most precious gift" is not life at any price, but the life of spiritual freedom and moral integrity. Her simple reply to Hale substantiates a point I have already made: "I think that be the Devil's argument." She believes this, but she cannot prove it: "I cannot dispute with you, sir; I lack learning for it"; and again, as in *St. Joan,* the learning of the scholars, the theologians, and the rulers is discredited, but not defeated, by the simple faith of a country woman.

The communication of this faith is Miller's best technical achievement in this play, for it depends very largely on his command of a new form of language specially adapted to the demands of his theme. Just as *St. Joan* (to draw one final parallel) is the most poetic of Shaw's plays, so the language of *The Crucible* is heightened in exactly similar ways. However, where Shaw gives Joan a country dialect largely for antiromantic and comic-realistic effect ("Where be Dauphin?" and "Thou art a rare noodle, Master"), the rustic-archaic speech of Miller's characters gives them such a natural eloquence and simple dignity that he does not need to abandon it as Shaw does in the more highly-charged situations but can (as my quotations will have shown) use it to good purpose throughout. It is simple and unpretentious, relying mainly on the use of unusual forms of the verb and on "Mister" as a form of address that becomes unexpectedly successful in its suggestion of an unsophisticated kind of antagonistic formality. Far from finding its quaintness disturbing in the theatre, I have been impressed by its self-controlled candour even on the lips of English actors, and it contributes significantly to the keynote of the play, which I have defined as one of conscientious endeavour in an uncertain world. There is a forthrightness about *The Crucible* that is well supported by its language as well as by its structural simplicity. . . .

Six months after the play's New York opening, Miller made some changes in the text, including the addition of a new scene, and critics are reported to have found the new version "more fluid, forceful and poetic." The changes mainly affected Proctor's part, making it more lyrical in Act II by the introduction of such lines as "Lilacs have a purple smell. Lilac is the smell of nightfall, I think." Similarly, in Act IV, his final speech to his wife had originally consisted simply of the exhortation "Give them no tear! Show a stony heart and sink them with it!"; the revision made him answer Hale (whom he had previously ignored) and expanded the speech as follows:

> *Hale.* Man, you will hang! You cannot!
> *Proctor* [*his eyes full of tears*]. I can. And there's your first marvel, that I can. You have made your magic now, for now I do think I see some shred of goodness in John Proctor. Not enough to weave a banner with, but white enough to keep it from such dogs. [*Elizabeth, in a burst of terror, rushes to him and weeps against his hand.*] Give them no tear! Tears pleasure them! Show honor now, show a stony heart and sink them with it!

It is not his heroism so much as his self-awareness that is increased by the change, just as his forthrightness had been emphasised by the introduction of the Cheever episode in Act III, as well as by minor additions elsewhere.

A less happy addition was a short scene in a wood, which was inserted before the trial scene. In it Proctor, on the eve of his wife's trial, meets Abigail to warn her of his intention to denounce her in court unless she abjures her denunciation of witches. Abigail, however, half-crazed with religious mania and with frustrated love for Proctor (of which she reminds him passionately), does not believe him:

> *Proctor.* . . . and you will never cry witchery again, or I will make you famous for the whore you are!
> *Abigail* [*she grabs him*]. Never in this world! I know you, John—you are this moment singing secret Hallelujahs that your wife will hang!
> *Proctor* [*throws her down*]. You mad, you murderous bitch!
> *Abigail.* . . . Fear naught. I will save you tomorrow. From yourself I will save you.

Obviously it is a powerful but quite superfluous scene, and Miller was wise to abandon it in subsequent editions. Its removal suggests, as I remarked earlier, that he is in two minds about Abigail, for in this scene her religiosity makes her more pathetically deluded than evil, so that the second thoughts which led him to cut it out may be connected with the desire to accentuate the element of evil. In any case, the past relationship between Proctor and Abby has been clearly established in the first two acts; Proctor's eyes have been opened to her true nature by the circumstances of his wife's arrest, after which he is hardly likely to seek a secret interview with her alone (if only for fear of being accused of interfering with a witness); and his disclosure of his intentions detracts from the dramatic power of the moment in Act III when he confesses his adultery. By the end of Act II, our attention has been effectively directed to Proctor, and the spotlight of the action is already narrowing into focus on his eventual clash with the court, so that we are becoming impatient of incidents that do not materially bear upon that. Thus this wood scene is an embarrassment, as is also the opening passage of Act IV, with Tituba and Sarah Good, which could easily be dispensed with as a distraction.

. . . In the very earliest version of the play, Miller seems to have reverted to the more extended manner of narration he was using before *All My Sons*: An opening scene set in a forest had to be abandoned because of the cost of building the set, but it is unlikely to have done much that is not better done in the final version by retrospective description. Something of the old realism still survives in some of the detailed settings and stage directions (at one point Danforth is even directed to blow his nose). Most interesting in this respect is Miller's preoccupation with the source of light in each scene. In Act I the sun streams through the leaded panes of a narrow window; in Act III sunlight pours through two high windows; in Act IV moonlight seeps through the bars of another high window. This may not be readily translatable into a lighting plot, but it shows how Miller sees the mood of the play—darkness and gloom penetrated by the single shaft of light cast by conscientiously dogged goodness. The revised version of July 1953, staged under Miller's own direction, "did away with all scenery, and had the action take place against drapes and a light-flooded cyclorama." The starkness of such a production would well suit the starkness of the play's theme, for it is a play that hovers on the brink of nihilism in a nightmare of lost innocence. . . .

No Play Is Deeper Than Its Witches

by Herbert Blau

. . . Even to this day, a revival of *The Crucible* will take up slack at the box office. Whatever that may be a sign of, in our theater there was no doubt the reign of McCarthy had a lot to do with its initial success. Miller, however, has tried to minimize the immediate parallel: "It was not only the rise of 'McCarthyism' that moved me, but something which seemed more weird and mysterious. It was the fact that a political, objective, knowledgeable campaign from the far Right was capable of creating not only a terror, but a new subjective reality, a veritable mystique which was gradually assuming even a holy resonance."

The mystique was resonating into an even more subtle shape than Miller had imagined. But while it lacked the terrifying impartiality of greater drama, *The Crucible* had nevertheless the vehemence of good social protest. The play was unevenly cast, put into rehearsal in haste (lest somebody take advantage of the release of rights before we did), the director was replaced after about three weeks, but the actors, upon whom the drama makes no special demands, played it with fervor and conviction if not subtlety. And in our program notes we stressed the McCarthy parallel, speaking of guilt by association and Ordeal by Slander.

The production made us a lot of liberal friends. They are all, all honorable men, but while I have signed the same petitions, that friendship in the theater has always been a little unsettling and subsequent plays have borne out my feeling that if we have the same politics, we do not always have it for the same reasons. While the power of mass psychosis is one of the strongest elements in the play, there is a melodrama in the fervency that always made me uncomfortable. When I brought it up, it made others uncomfortable. But I think it behooves us to understand both the appeal and limitations of this forceful drama—one of those which seems effective so long as it is even middlingly well played, and despite its fate on Broadway.

The Puritan community, as Hawthorne knew in *The Scarlet Letter,* is the ideal setting for a realistic narrative of allegorical dimensions. As Miller puts it, drawing on the annals of the Salem trials: "To write a realistic play of that world was already to write in a style beyond contemporary realism." And there is a powerful admonition beyond that in Proctor's final refusal to be *used.* Like Miller before the congressional committee, he will not lend his name to the naming of names. On this level the play has authority, and it serves as an exemplum. Several critics have pointed out that the analogy between witches and Communists is a weak one, for while we believe in retrospect there were no witches, we know in fact there were some Communists, and a few of them were dangerous. (If Miller were another kind of dramatist, he might claim there *were* witches, but we shall come to that in a moment.) Yet as a generalization, the play's argument is worthy; as a warning against "the handing over of conscience," it is urgent; and to the extent his own public life has re-required it, Miller has shown the courage of his convictions beyond most men—and hence has some right to call for it. One might still wish he were more inventive in form, but in a period where the borders between art and anarchy are ill-defined, we might apply the caution stated in II Corinthians: "All things are lawful, but not all things edify." It is no small thing to say *The Crucible* is an edifying drama.

What the play does not render, however, is what Miller claims for it and what is deeply brooding in the Puritan setting: "the interior psychological question," the harrowing descent of mass hallucination into the life of the individual, where value is deranged, no reason is right, and every man drives his bargain with the sinister. One sees this in *The Brothers Karamazov,* which Miller invokes as that "great book of wonder," and more relevantly in *The Possessed,* where political evil is the reptilian shadow of indecipherable sin. For Proctor, a sin is *arranged*, so that his guilt might have cause. All we can say is: that is not the way it is. For Miller, a psychosis is no more than a psychosis, with clear motive and rational geography. The symptoms are fully describable. His love of wonder is deflated by his desire "to write rationally" and to put a judgmental finger on "the full loathsomeness of . . . anti-social action." The desire is admirable, but the danger is to locate it in advance. Studying Dostoyevsky, Miller had resolved to "let wonder rise up like a mist, a gas, a vapor from the gradual and remorseless crush of factual and psychological conflict." But while that is a good description of the source of wonder in Dostoyevsky, Miller is restive in the mist, which in Dostoyevsky is thickened to nightmare by every wincing judgment and every laceration of meaning, writhing in the imminence of wrong.

By contrast, we know only too well what *The Crucible* means, nor were the issues really ever in doubt. Wanting to write a drama "that would lift out of the morass of subjectivism the squirming, single, defined process" by which public terror unmans us, Miller fills in the record with the adultery of John Proctor and Abigail Williams. He thus provides the rationalist's missing link to the mystery of the crying out. The adultery brings the drama back toward the "subjectivism" Miller was trying to avoid, but its real subjective life remains shallow. Taking up charges of coldness, he says he had never written more passionately and blames the American theater—actors, directors, audience, and critics—for being trained "to take to heart anything that does not prick the mind and to suspect everything that does not supinely reassure."

About the American theater, I think this is exactly so. But my own reservations have to do with the fact that, while moral instruction may be a legitimate ambition of the drama, the play *does* reassure— and it is the *mind* which rebels *finally* against its formulas while the emotions may be overwhelmed by its force. A play is privileged to reconstruct history for its own purposes; but here we have a play which pretends to describe in realistic terms a community instinctively bent on devotion to God. The Puritans were readers of signs, and the signs, in daily behavior, were evidences of God's will. Hawthorne's novel retains the impermeable quality of that experience by accepting completely the terms of the divine or demonic game. It is

yours to choose whose game it really is, according to his strategy of
alternative possibilities. But Miller's play makes the choices for you,
and its hero does not stand—as one approving critic has said—"four-
square in his own time and place." The records do show that he considered the inquisition a fraud; but though he is bound to the community as a farmer, he does not, in Miller's play, take to heart "all
the complex tensions of the Salem community," for he responds to
things like an eighteenth century rationalist with little stake in established doctrine. Truer to time and place is the Reverend Hale, who
knew "the devil is precise" and saw him in the godly, in himself. He
is certainly the more dramatic figure in being compelled to disavow
what by instinct and conditioning he has come to believe. Hale resembles Captain Vere in Melville's *Billy Budd,* where the drama is
truly divested of "subjectivism" by characters who are, by *allegiance*
to retarded doctrine, impaled upon the cross of choice.

One can also see in Melville's Claggart the kind of character that
Miller now wishes he had portrayed in Danforth: evil embodied to
the utmost, a man so dedicated to evil that by his nature we might
know good. Melville saw that to create such a character he would
have to stretch his skepticism toward the ancient doctrine of "depravity according to nature," which alone could explain a Claggart
or an Iago. He does this by a strategy of insinuation. He suggests to
us that there was once such a doctrine, in which intelligent modern
men, of course, can hardly believe. The story virtually drives us back
to the "superstition," as Kafka virtually restores Original Sin. (I
should add that Melville does this in the prose style of the novelette,
which could not always be compensated for in the admirable
dramatization by Coxe and Chapman.) Doing so, he takes us back
through time, justifying as far as form can reach the eternal intima-
tions of Billy's rosy-dawned execution; a scene which is almost
enough to make you believe, with the sailors, that a chip of the
dockyard boom "was a piece of the Cross."

Almost. Having proposed to us a possibility just over the edge of
reason, Melville writes an ironic coda in which he leaves us to take
our own risks of interpretation. Miller, for all his moral conviction
and belief in free choice, leaves us none. A master of conventional
dramaturgy, with all the skills of building and pacing, he drives past
the turbid aspect of social hypnosis to the predetermined heroism of

Proctor. Perception yields to sensation and the choice of classical tragedy to its wish-fulfillment. (It is curious that Billy, *typed* down to his stammer, is a more inscrutable character than anyone in Miller's play.) The final irony is that John Proctor, dramatic hero of the populist mind, might even be applauded by members of the congressional committee that cited Miller for contempt. It is no accident, too, that in temperament and general conduct Proctor resembles our true culture hero, John Glenn, who would be perfectly cast for the role if the astronauts were to start a little theater. One may not have the courage to be a Proctor at the final drumroll, nor a Glenn at the countdown, but no one doubts they are worthy of imitation.

This absence of doubt reduced the import of *The Crucible* for those who thought about it, while increasing the impact for those who didn't. You do a play for its virtues, and one devious aspect of the art of theater lies in concealing the faults. Actually, my belief is that if you know what's not there, you can deal more powerfully with what is. Little of what I have said, however, came up during rehearsals of *The Crucible* (which was not so much conceived as put on), but rather in critiques and discussions of plays done later. Whatever its weaknesses, the production was hard-driving in keeping with the play's rhythm, and performance by performance the actors rose to overwhelming approval. Because we would be doing better productions which would not be so approved, it was important to keep our heads. And, indeed, I think this attitude has made it more possible for our actors to sustain their belief through more subtle plays that have not been so vigorously applauded.

At the time we produced *The Crucible,* Miller was already the most powerful rational voice in the American theater. Questioning the play later, I wanted the company to understand that to criticize him was to take his ideas seriously, and to begin to give some shape to our own. The people we often had to question most were those with whom we seemed to agree. Because we were all vulnerable to easy judgments and that depth psychology of the surface which is so inherent in American drama (and acting), it was necessary to see why *The Crucible* was not really the "tough" play that Miller claimed; I mean dramatically tough, tough in soul, driving below its partisanship to a judgment of antisocial action from which, as in

Dostoyevsky, none of us could feel exempt. I wouldn't have asked the questions if Miller didn't prompt them with his reflections on Social Drama and the tragic form. But compare the action of Proctor to that of the tragic figures of any age—Macbeth, or Brittanicus, or Raskolnikov: Can you approve or disapprove of their action? Can you make the choice of imitating them? Or avoid it? *The Crucible* may confirm what we like to think we believe, but it is not, as Miller says, intimidating to an "Anglo-Saxon audience" (or actors), nor does it really shock us into recognizing that we don't believe what we say we do. Beyond that, the profoundest dramas shake up our beliefs, rock our world; in *The Crucible,* our principles are neither jeopardized nor extended, however much we may fail to live by them anyhow.

As for the inquisitors, Miller wants us to see evil naked and unmitigated. I am prepared to believe it exists (I am certain it exists), and I won't even ask where it comes from. But—to be truer than tough—if you want absolute evil, you've got to think more about witches. Miller wants the Puritan community without Puritan premises or Puritan intuitions (which is one reason why, when he appropriates the language, his own suffers in comparison). His liberalism is the kind that, really believing we have outlived the past, thinks it is there to be used. The past just doesn't lie around like that. And one of these days the American theater is really going to have to come to terms with American history.

Axion for liberals: No play is deeper than its witches. . . .

Setting, Language, and the Force of Evil in *The Crucible*

by Penelope Curtis

. . . Although other plays by Miller are more overtly based on Greek models, *The Crucible* is the only one in which a whole community is directly, and tragically, implicated; it is, I realize, an almost impossible achievement for plays with a modern setting (hence the comparative futility of "modernizing" Greek models at all, whether the dramatist is Anouilh or O'Neill or Miller himself), but it is a tremendous strength in *The Crucible*; it bears directly on the dramatizing of forces. . . .

By "community" I mean, of course, something very much more than common social factors of the kind we see in, say, *A View from the Bridge*: area, class, occupation, certain habits of life, a few slang words, and the simple code that a man must not "snitch." Insofar as these represent the life of a community, that life is an impoverished one. But in any case, only individuals are *directly* implicated in what happens to Eddie. In this respect, *The Crucible* is closer in spirit to Sophoclean drama; for the fate of the Salem people actually depends, to a lesser or greater extent, on the choices of individual men. There's more diversity in *The Crucible* than, say, in *Oedipus Rex*, a wider range of individual choices (it covers Hale *and* Abigail *and* Putnam, as well as Proctor), but the principle is similar. And the fate of the community involves more than the physical life or death of its members: There is a metaphysic at stake, and a way of life; the reputation of a people which becomes, by extension, an

---

image of human possibilities. As with the Greek *polis,* every aspect
of life was involved in the whole; but Salem being the kind of theocracy it was, the pressure of involvement was greater to an unnatural
degree. It is interesting to see at what point, in each case, community life becomes significant. In both plays, drama occurs at the
meeting point of divine and secular law: in a personal ruler in the
one, and the religious courts in the other. In *Oedipus Rex,* however,
there was a second figure of authority in the prophet Teiresias; but
in Salem there was, in the crucial period, no court of appeal. Hence
there were greater possibilities of moral disaster *in the community
itself.*

Clearly when John Proctor speaks about his "name," it has a much
denser meaning than when Eddie speaks of his. The Salem community was so closely knit that there was constant difficulty in distin-
guishing salvation from personal integrity, reputation, prestige, fac-
tional power, and selfish pride. The language of the play reveals a
shifting preoccupation with all of these, in such a way as to suggest
how the nature of the drama arises from the nature of the community.

As Miller points out, the two crucial factors in their lives were
the land and their religion. So powerfully did these unite them that
he was able to give his characters an expressive, wide-ranging idiom
that draws continuously on both sources. Their speech has the salti-
ness, the physicality, of a life lived close to the soil and the waste;
it is enriched, too, by a literary influence that has likewise been
assimilated into daily life: the Bible, partly mediated by a seventeenth-century sermon convention. From both, it draws a quality of
passion. Take, for instance, an early speech of Proctor's:

> Learn charity, woman. I have gone tiptoe in this house all seven
> month since she is gone. I have not moved from there to there with-
> out I think to please you, and still an everlasting funeral marches
> round your heart. . . .

The phrasing is harsh ("without I think . . ."), but very physically
suggestive, and its suggestiveness is suddenly embodied in that piece
of highly individual rhetoric: "still an everlasting funeral marches
round your heart." The emotion is Proctor's own; the tone of right-
eous fury comes from the pulpit tradition.

Or take this much later speech of Elizabeth's to him:

> I have read my heart this three month, John. I have sins of my own
> to count. It needs a cold wife to prompt lechery.

The rhetoric of this is less obviously individual. The language
comes more directly from the common ethic ("read my heart," "sins,"
"lechery"), yet the cadences are quite movingly her own: "this three
month, John," "a cold wife," and again we find an instinctively
physical quality in the language—as in that word "prompt." Miller
has not merely borrowed an idiom; he has given it considerable
range, using it to distinguish different voices, different qualities of
emotion, as well as to suggest the common sources of their lives.
Proctor's speech is impressive, and certainly felt, but it has an element of bombast by comparison with the later one by Elizabeth.
And the greater sincerity of her statement reflects, quite directly,
the spiritual maturing they have both experienced in the course of
the play. . . .

The language is not just compressed; it has a muscularity which
enforces the meaning. "I have fought here three long years to bend
these stiff-necked people to me": Parris is "stiff-necked," too—it
comes out in his harsh, determined, fearful speech, together with the
resistance offered by "these people." There is a lively play of half-
metaphor that suggests several things at once about his preoccupations, and those of the community. What is obstinacy in others is
"upright" in himself and his own; and we can sense, in the blend
of ugliness and resonance in his language, just how far he is typical
of the others, and how far his feelings are extreme ones.

The play of what I have called "half-metaphor" is the staple of
the dialogue, and helps immensely to suggest the implications of
what this or that character says so tersely. "There be no blush about
my name," says Abigail, when she is asked if it is "entirely white."
Both she and Elizabeth Proctor understand the idea of a "white"
name, but Abigail sees the impediment to it in terms of her own
hot blood, in terms of personal humiliation. Goody Proctor uses a
different expression: "She will not sit so close to something soiled."
There is just as much feeling, just as much physicality; but *she* sees
the impediment in terms of a moral pollution that deprives the
sinner of human status: "*something* soiled." These half-developed

metaphors are continually used to suggest (though not, in the Shake-spearian sense, to create) the themes of the play; and while one should not pause too long over the associations—if one tries to bring the implications of "blush," "something soiled," and "I will not black my face" into too direct a relationship, the dialogue will start to fall apart—the language seems to me to avoid all dangers of quaintness or artificiality: not only in its cadences, but in the muscular way it keeps the Salem preoccupations and prejudices alive in our minds.

Clearly, then, *The Crucible* is a work of some subtlety and range, and I hope I have already offered reasons for seeing it as unusual—in language and setting alone—among Miller's plays. To show *how* unusual, one must look at the whole course of events, and above all at the court scenes. For these scenes make an overwhelming impression when the play is staged, and yet the popular reading, which takes *The Crucible* to be one "tragedy" of several by that famous writer Arthur Miller, almost entirely fails to account for them. The phrase "mass hysteria" cannot by itself do the work. Even now, most people seem to read the play in the way first indicated by the commentary, and suggested, to a lesser extent, by the recurrent feeling that McCarthyism somehow offered an historical "perspective" on it: seeing the play as being (in the words of Richard Watts, Jr.) about "the free man's courageous and never-ending fight against mass pressures to make him bow down in conformity." . . .

But the play takes a completely, and significantly, different course from this. There are signs of witchcraft, but they are found in the camp of those who later become the persecutors. The Reverend Parris, and the girls, are in their several ways fearful for their *own* safety. Even the poppet later found in Elizabeth's house belongs, in fact, to Mary Warren, and it is Abigail who sticks the pin in it. Together such details form a pattern which might seem overemphasized if it were not for the fact that it is generally overlooked. The pattern is ironic, to say the least. Yet the play is not at all ironic in tone or in its best-timed theatrical effects—which is, perhaps, its greatest difference from Shaw's play [*St. Joan*]. *The Crucible* is so charged, so immediate, that it does not stop—at least for the first three acts—to take historical, or any other perspectives. I am not suggesting, of course, that Abigail and Mary Warren are themselves conventional witches, that the play endorses the Salem metaphysic while inverting its action. But even if we insist that witched children, poppets stuck with needles, and so on, are signs of the Devil to the seventeenth-century mind rather than to our own, they do, I think, give some external points of reference, and disturbing ones, for that sense of evil forces generated in the play by quite other means.

Our very first stage-impression is of a child lying on a bed, who, though immovably asleep, cries at the name of the Lord, attempts to fly, and so on. And while there are all sorts of possible explanations, familiar psychological ones, the play does not in fact give them. Only Rebecca Nurse is able to declare that there is no witchcraft here, that "she'll wake when she tires of it." But Goody Nurse herself carries such an impressive burden of innocence, of positive goodness, that it is hard to say that she is simply giving a rational explanation. One feels that when she enters and sits by the child ("who gradually quiets"), she is opposing herself, the quality of being she brings with her, to whatever it is that is upsetting the adults and keeping the child in an unnatural condition. When she says, "A child's spirit is like a child, you can never catch it by running after it; you must stand still, and, *for love,* it will soon itself come back" (my italics), she herself names a motive which can also be, and in her own case is, a force. The effect of her entry is subtly to engage us in a situation which, however unreal it seems at first, is seen progressively as more complex and disturbing. With the uncovering of the *practices* of "witchcraft" (and these are unmistakable: naked dancing, frogs, drinking blood, and conjuring of spirits), at least two foci of human malice are discovered, one of them in a middle-aged woman. And as more people gather, other, less readily identifiable, warnings are sounded, as in the Putnam-Proctor exchange: "I am sick of meetings; cannot the man turn his head without he have a meeting?" "He may turn his head, but not to Hell!"; or again, in Rebecca Nurse's sanity, "There is prodigious danger in the seeking of loose spirits. I fear it, I fear it. Let us rather blame ourselves . . ." But before the courts are instituted, malice and accusation have insignificant power. There is the promise of worse to come, in the way Abigail's private acts of bullying lead into the semipublic scene where Tituba is accused and "forgiven"—a small drama prefiguring the larger one. But where her social equals are concerned, Proctor's usual toughness and forthrightness are quite equal to threats made out of court. What these rumours and preliminary disturbances do accomplish is to expose the weaknesses in the community and its various members, through which the forces of evil will later act.

Evil with a capital "E" comes into power only when the community gives it institutional status; when in the words of Danforth, "the entire contention of the State in these trials is that the voice of Heaven is speaking through the children"; when the community surrenders the sacred power over life and death to the hands of a corrupt judge and a group of hysterical or malicious girls. And Evil with a capital "E" can be rendered on stage only by the metaphoric quality of the speeches (as in *Macbeth*), or as here when the fever of malice can be visibly transmitted from one person to another in public. For this is what happens in the court scenes. . . .

But if the procedure is relentless, it's by no means predictable. For one thing, there's a considerable range of personalities and claims, a powerful, if choked, resistance. For another, there is the peculiarly rhetorical nature of the evidence, and the extraordinary dynamism latent in large gatherings of people. Mary cannot faint at will; her crime is not really her own, so her powers are not at her own disposal. Her inability to faint marks the impossibility of disproving the evidence by facts. But in any case, it was never really that kind of evidence: it is the evidence of *personal testimony*. And as such, it can be "disproved" only by a more forceful testimony, by a more persuasive force of personal conviction. Hence the procedure is that of men *declaring* their evidence, proving their case by the force of their sincerity. And when "sincerity" becomes the criterion for a communal judgment, one finds released into the situation all the power of mixed or false motives, all the force of the human need to be justified. When I say one finds this power "released," I mean that the dialogue pulsates with it, every speech is filled with the ring of this or that man's conviction. The excitement, the sense of crisis, communicates itself over a whole variety of rhetorical certainties, from Danforth's "I tell you straight, Mister—I have seen marvels in this court. I have seen people choked before my eyes by spirits; I have seen them stuck by pins and slashed by daggers," to Giles's "helpless sobs" . . . "I have broke charity with the woman, I have broke charity with her." Such a conflict can be won only by the side which adapts itself to, and makes use of, this condition of excitement, of rhetorical excess. And yet it is precisely such excess that Proctor sets himself against. He cannot convince, because he cannot fully abandon himself to his own rhetoric. He is at once too controlled and too little calculating.

It is obvious that the nature of the court, and hence of its evidence, lends itself very directly to a stage convention. My second point is even more closely connected with the staging: that where one tense scene dissolves, it leaves a gap which can be filled by an even greater tension; or to put it another way, a state of excitement can be generated among a gathering of people which is quite out of proportion to the individual emotions, and which, like fire, can leap incalculable distances. This is a basic principle of drama (being, among other things, a matter of timing), and it has come to be a truism of mass psychology; but I do not know any other play which makes quite such conscious and electrifying use of it or which allows the principle to appropriate quite such implications in a moral struggle. The crucial scene begins [p. 108] when Elizabeth is called in, and ends with Mary Warren's capitulation. . . .

The pacing is careful, not rushed. The dialogue retains its qualities of irony, even of humour ("Envy is a deadly sin, Mary") and sane protest; yet even these are made to serve, by delaying, and heightening, a quite different total effect. After the tension and the waiting, Elizabeth's brave lie comes *dramatically* as a kind of moral collapse, leaving a vacuum which is therefore able to be filled by Abby, and the force that sweeps through her and the others is overpowering. Even the stage directions become permeated with it (*"Danforth, himself engaged and entered by Abigail"*); and by the time the girls are fully under the influence of Abigail, or of that power which she temporarily represents, we too look up expecting to see the yellow bird in the rafters. But if we do so, it is not that we are momentarily convinced by her lies, and look towards the rafters for Mary Warren's naughty spirit; it is not that kind of optical, or moral, delusion. It is because we feel the presence of a malevolent power so great it might easily reveal itself as a terrible yellow bird. And the malevolence shows in the ugly effect the girls' screaming has on Mary, with her own prolonged scream, her finger pointing, and her "Abby, Abby, I'll never hurt you more!"

If the climax of the play lies in this conflict, and the triumph of evil, the play as a whole is in some kind of tragic "mode," with Proctor as hero—which makes for a certain imbalance. There is a process, however shadowy and incomplete, from the fierce drama culminating in Act III to a simpler, more nearly self-righteous, "Proctor-tragedy"; and this process can be traced in the movements of the subplot. For the Proctor-Proctor-Williams triangle, like Proctor himself, is given somewhat different emphasis from the rest of the play—a more modern emphasis. While the private drama parallels the wider, more important conflict in the community, the terms of the choice are differently experienced. There is a tension between the kind of exchange we hear between Proctor and Abigail, in their first scene together, where we find not merely physical awareness, but, I think, some passion ("I have a sense for heat, John, and yours has drawn me to my window . . ."), and the growing relationship between Elizabeth and John, which is passionate in another way. *They* share a passionate desire for trust and wholeness, for a mutual growth in self-knowledge, which is brought (despite doubts and reticences) to an apotheosis in Elizabeth's speech: "I have read my heart this three month, John. I have sins of my own to count. It needs a cold wife to prompt lechery. . . ." The crucial difference between this sexual conflict and the larger, more metaphysical one, is that here Abby, in her simple human aspect, has some value: inferior to Elizabeth's in that she is not capable of growth, but nevertheless showing a fierce sense of deprivation which merits, at the least, our sympathy. Both women use the name "John" with a love that is almost visible.

So long as the sexual triangle qualifies and deepens the main drama, well and good; but there comes a time when it may threaten to supersede it. Abby, as a member of the triangle, is nothing—or rather, she acts powerfully on circumstances, but as a figure of interest she is soon forgotten. On the other hand our growing involvement in the relationship between John and Elizabeth may warn us of a change of emphasis. It is not simply that the play wanders from the Aristotelian ideal, by making so much depend on something incalculable, almost a trick. After all, it never really followed the Aristotelian pattern; tricks, unexpectedness, decisions of the moment, are essential to the drama in Act III. It is rather that, as Proctor's dilemma comes to the fore, its representative nature seems less and less clear. Elizabeth's lie—the true pivot of the play—is felt dramatically as a failure and a miscalculation; but not because it was morally wrong. For the first time, the drama and the moral issues seem to diverge. In so far as Rebecca Nurse and her friends represent the polarized "good" (and up till now they have done so), the question put to Elizabeth represents, at this point, an absolute moral test; if she should tell the truth, both Proctor's freedom and some kind of communal regeneration would be likely to follow. But in the excitement of the moment we think only of Proctor. The dramatic emphasis invites us to hope, not that Elizabeth should make the morally uncompromising decision, but that her husband should be spared decision altogether. It is odd to find this weakness at the high point of the play, yet I would maintain it is there. Certainly the collapse after her lie allows for the full force of the "crying out"; but by the time the question of absolute decision is revived, the play has partly changed its character, and Proctor is noticeably a less representative figure. There is a shift of attention, effected here, but felt more fully later, from the struggle of forces in a community to a private tension of feeling.

The moment when Elizabeth lies and condemns Proctor marks a further shift of attention: from John's relationship with his wife to his relationship with himself. From this point the stress falls more and more, not on his representative dilemma, suffering, a choice, though these remain in view, but rather on his representative personality. And it is here that Miller almost falters. Proctor is unlike his usual, carefully objectified, "little men" heroes, and he is a much more satisfactory full-scale hero than the crass mouthpiece of *After the Fall*; the trouble lies, perhaps, in Proctor's being so very unobjectionable to twentieth-century prejudices and taste. He has all the sceptical virtues, together with a guilty conscience and an upright heart, and in creating him Miller comes closest to writing the play he seems to have intended. Certainly, for the first three acts, Proctor is satisfactorily handled as one strong member in a complex drama;

as independent "chooser" he is adequately related to that polarization of "good" and "evil" characters which Richard Watts finds too simple, but which is in my opinion crucial to the *seen* metaphysical conflict. Towards the end, though, Proctor seems to be imaginatively detached from the other Salem "accused," even from the accusers, in a way which is partly a distraction. There are moments when he speaks out of context, as a man faced with an archetypal, but *abstract,* dilemma. "Because it is my name!" he cries, "Because I cannot have another in my life . . ."; and again, "I can. And there's your first marvel, that I can. You have made your magic now, for now I do think I see some shred of goodness in John Proctor." These are moving statements. They *are* related to the moral life of the community, and they will affect the other innocent accused; they are infused with metaphysical concepts; and there is a force of conviction which partly goes to meet the previous displays of hysteria, meet something of the expectations raised by "God's icy wind will blow." And yet, here as nowhere else, John Proctor's "name" and his "goodness" seem to come forward from their context and take on a more familiar twentieth-century meaning—or, perhaps, a generalized, simplified meaning—but by way of a recognizably modern device. The words "magic" and "marvel" seem to have inverted commas around them. Indeed, it is only under pressure of the final scenes that we fully realize he does not believe in "heaven" in the way his friends do. It is to some extent a different choice for him and for them. . . .

Historical Analogy and *The Crucible*

by Henry Popkin

. . . If we were not able to point out that the historical parallel in *The Crucible* is imperfect, we might still justifiably object that the impact of a sudden and undeserved punishment upon entirely innocent people is a difficult subject for drama. Aristotle's criticism of the entirely blameless hero continues to be valid. In apparent recognition of this principle, Miller has constructed a new sort of guilt for his hero, John Proctor. In the play, Proctor has been unfaithful to his wife, and Miller goes out of his way to assure us directly that his infidelity violates his personal code of behavior. The girl whom he loved, jealous and resentful of being rejected, accuses Proctor's wife of witchcraft, and so Proctor, who has, in this peculiar fashion, caused his wife to be accused, has a special obligation to save her. In trying to save her, he is himself charged with witchcraft. So, he does suffer for his guilt—but for a different guilt, for adultery, not for witchcraft.

But it must be remembered that a play is not merely an exercise in ideas or even in characterization. It is a creation that moves forward in time, catching interest and creating suspense. While the historical context is useful to any preliminary understanding of a play, any full understanding and any proper evaluation must follow a close look at its plot. The plot presents to us an ebb and flow of argument and incident, an alternation of crises, turning, in *The Crucible,* about the issue of witchcraft.

The Crucible begins with a crisis, a moment of excitement that shows the false witnesses in full cry—one child on stage and another

"Historical Analogy and *The Crucible*" [editor's title] by Henry Popkin. From "*Arthur Miller's* The Crucible," College English, 26 (*November 1964*), *139–46.* Copyright © *1964 by the National Council of Teachers of English. Reprinted by permission of the publisher and Henry Popkin.*

of whom we are told, both of them displaying the different but
equally convincing symptoms of demonic possession. We note a
number of fatuous adult responses to the children's behavior, and
then the adults conveniently leave the stage to the children, who
effectively clear up any mysteries by frankly discussing their deceit-
ful actions. They incidentally, and very usefully, provide us with
Abigail's special motive, her jealous hatred of Elizabeth Proctor. Directly upon this cue, John Proctor enters, and, perhaps a bit im-
probably revealing too many intimate secrets in the presence of a
child feigning possession, he and Abigail tell us most of what we
need to know about their love affair and its present consequences.
In quick succession, then, we have seen the central disorder of the
play, demonic possession, and the explanation for it; in the children's malice, we have also noted a particular form of malice that
is to breed results to come—Abigail's jealousy. The main exposition
has been effected, and the main lines of action are ready.

At once the skeptic, Proctor, clashes with Parris, the believer in
witchcraft. The argument between the skeptical and the credulous,
and the ensuing effort to convince the community dominate all of
the play. Like other works by Miller, *The Crucible* has something of
the quality of a trial, of a court case, even before the formal hearings
begin. Throughout, the exponents of both views are arguing their
cases, making their points, and, inadvertently, revealing their real
motives. Proctor and Parris now engage in just such a dispute, showing us their own personal hostility and helpfully bringing in some
additional exposition concerning the land war, the rivalry over min-
isterial appointments, and the issue of Parris's salary. These are the
real, underlying issues that motivate the men of Salem.

Once the local prejudices have been established, we have reached
the appropriate moment for the arrival of the guileless outsider, the
idealistic seeker of witches, John Hale. In theory, Hale is perfectly
equipped to combat witchcraft, and he even enters carrying visible
evidence of his qualifications, the heavy books that have enlightened
him. In practice, he is as helpless as a child, much more helpless than
the children of the play. He is totally unequipped, precisely because
he is an outsider with a load of irrelevant academic knowledge, precisely because he has missed the informative conversations that just
precede his entrance. He has pursued the wrong study; instead of

demonology, he should have applied himself to economics, the psychopathology of children, and eavesdropping. Hale is the simple, eager man of good will, the human *tabula rasa* upon whom the experience of the play will write. His simplicity makes him the ideal audience for the wholesale charges of witchcraft that begin to be made as the curtain falls upon the first act. As we should expect, these charges proceed inevitably from the circumstances that the previous action has painstakingly interpreted.

After some preliminary exposition of the cool relationship between John Proctor and his wife, the second act provides, in order, Elizabeth Proctor's interrogation of her husband, the Proctors' joint interrogation of Mary Warren, and, finally, the real goal of the scene —Hale's examination of the Proctors. One incidental effect of this repeated use of courtroom technique is to show us that Elizabeth Proctor's justice to her husband is as lacking in mercy and understanding as the public justice of Salem. The crime of adultery that Elizabeth continues to probe and to worry over has already been adequately punished and repented for, but Elizabeth will never permit herself to forget it.

Following the troubled exchange between the Proctors comes the only courtroom procedure that brings out the truth, the Proctors' joint examination of Mary Warren. A suitable rigor on the part of the questioners and the threat of a whipping bring the whole truth out of her fast enough. Then Hale takes the initiative, less successfully. He is a sufficiently experienced investigator to hunt out a crime, but, without knowing it, he has found the wrong crime—adultery, not witchcraft. He causes Proctor to miss the seventh commandment and evidently takes that failure as a sign of the man's general impiety when it is really a sort of Freudian slip, an unwilling confession of his infidelity. In addition, Hale rightly sniffs out the general atmosphere of guilt and notes "some secret blasphemy that stinks to Heaven." He is responding to the chilly atmosphere that Elizabeth Proctor maintains and to the shame that it produces in John Proctor. His suspicion has an ironically appropriate result: it is Elizabeth herself who is the victim of her own heavy insistence on the reality of guilt. In a sense, Hale is right to arrest her. She is guilty of pharisaism, which is a more serious charge than witchcraft or adultery, and Miller gives the unmistakable impression that he considers pharisaism a very serious offense indeed. (Pharisaism appears again and is again made to seem obnoxious in a later play of Miller's, *After the Fall,* where it is once more the trait of a wife whose husband has been unfaithful.)

The third act revolves about John Proctor's effort to save his wife; when the accusation is at last directed against him, the principal forward action of the play has come to an end. The charges of witchcraft have begun by hitting out blindly in all directions, but then, in accordance with the painstaking preparations that informed us of Abigail's jealousy of Elizabeth, the accusations fix upon Elizabeth. Proctor tries to reverse them by charging Abigail with adultery, but, in consequence, he is himself accused of witchcraft. Up to this time, slander has been spreading in all directions, attaching itself at random to one innocent victim after another, but now it finds its true and proper target. The real, the ultimate victim in this play is John Proctor, the one independent man, the one skeptic who sees through the witchcraft "craze" from the first. As if instinctively, in self-defense, the witchcraft epidemic has attacked its principal enemy. This is a climactic moment, a turning point in the play. New witches may continue to be named, but *The Crucible* now narrows its focus to John Proctor, caught in the trap, destroyed by his effort to save his wife, threatened by the irrationality that only he has comprehended.

The third act has an incidental function; it is climactic for Hale as well as for Proctor. Hale first appears as a zealous specialist; in the second act, he is shown going industriously about his work; in the third act, shaken by the obvious injustice of what he has brought to pass, he denounces the hearings. That is the crucial step for him, and, from that moment, his personal drama does not take any new direction, just as the general development of the play takes no distinctive new steps following these turning points for Proctor and Hale.

In addition, the third act is a carefully organized unit of argument and counterargument. Concerned to protect their authority, the judges promise a long period of safety for Elizabeth Proctor, and, when this stratagem fails, they start bullying the turncoat Mary Warren. Proctor counterattacks with the same low tactics that his enemies use—charging Abigail, the primary accuser, with the crimes that do her reputation the most damage; they are specifically anti-Puritan crimes, laughing during prayer and dancing. These are curious accusations from a skeptic, but he is learning, too late, to play his enemies' game. Abigail responds by attributing witchcraft to Mary Warren. This give-and-take continues when Proctor calls out "Whore! Whore!" After three acts of fencing, the real truth is out; the burden of establishing it rests with the one person whose truthfulness can be fully guaranteed—Elizabeth Proctor. All attention goes to her as she is asked the critical question. And, for once, in a moment of high excitement and suspense, this model of truthfulness lies because she values something more than the truth—her husband's good name.

The value Salem attributes to a good name has been indicated previously in the play; it becomes critically important in the last act. From the beginning, Salem has been presented as a community in which mutual evaluation is a generally popular activity. Prying, slander, and recrimination are unpleasant but persuasive testimonials to the value that attaches to a good name. Living in this environment and sharing its values, Elizabeth Proctor must value reputation even more than truth. This decision has disastrous results, for Mary Warren, facing serious punishment as a turncoat and possible witch, must defend herself by making a new charge—against the man who got her into this sorry mess, John Proctor. The path of the accusations has been circuitous, but Proctor is, in effect, being punished for his hostility to Salem's obsession with sin—in particular, his wife's obsession with adultery and the community's obsession with witchcraft. We may suspect a tacit hint that the two fixations are closely linked.

In the last act, public opinion has shifted: Andover is in revolt, even Parris is shaken, and more pressure is being applied to obtain confessions. Proctor can be saved only by a dishonest confession to witchcraft. Life is sufficiently dear for him to make the confession, but he will not let it become a public document. The issue is, once again, his good name. Previously preferred over truth, his good name is now preferred to life itself. This issue seems now to dominate the play, but, as we have observed, it has been prominent throughout, for accusations of witchcraft are harmful to the reputation as well as to the individual life. The citizens of Salem have been concerned

with scoring points against one another, with establishing their own
superior virtue and the depraved character of their enemies. To use
the word "depraved" is to remind ourselves that this state of affairs
is well suited to the Puritan theology, which held that divine election was the one balm for innate human depravity. Reputation
served as an indispensable guide to the state of grace, for it was an
outward sign of election. As a result, Proctor is not only expressing
a characteristically modern concern for his good name, a concern
equally important to the twentieth-century protagonist of Miller's
next full-length play, *A View from the Bridge*; he is exhibiting a
typically Puritan state of mind.

Proctor dies, then, for his good name; but to return to the troubling issue, his good name was not, in the most serious sense, threatened by the charges brought against him. His good name was, in
fact, being threatened by his fear of death and by his knowledge of
his own adultery, but it was shaken only in the most superficial way
by the charge of witchcraft. Proctor is not merely innocent; he is *an*
innocent, and his guilt as an adulterer is irrelevant, except insofar
as it supplies Abigail with her motive for slandering his wife. We
can see why Proctor's adultery had to be invented; surely it came
into existence because Miller found himself compelled to acknowl-
edge the Aristotelian idea that the blameless, unspotted hero is an
inadequate protagonist for a serious play.

This problem may be further illuminated by reference to some of
Miller's other works. In his first two Broadway successes, a relatively
unsullied hero (played in each case by an actor named Arthur Kennedy) is present, but he does not have the leading role. The chief
character in each of these plays, *All My Sons* and *Death of a Salesman,* is a guilty older man, who has lived by the wrong values. In
this last respect at least, he resembles Hale of *The Crucible,* but he
is more complex and more serious. Now, however, in *The Crucible,*
the younger, unsullied hero (again played in the original production
by Arthur Kennedy) moves into the foreground. Of course, Proctor
is deeply conscious of his infidelity to his wife, but this fact does not
affect his fundamental freedom from guilt; in a sense, he is unsullied, significantly less guilty than the sinful older men of the earlier
plays. We are obviously expected to apply a modern "psychological"
judgment to him and say that he was driven to adultery by a cold

wife and by the irresistible attraction of the conscienceless girl who seduced him. Abigail is not made "a strikingly beautiful girl" (in the stage directions) for nothing. We must exonerate Proctor, just as we are required to exonerate a similar character in a later play by Miller, another man who stands between a cold, complaining wife and an irresistible child-woman—Quentin in *After the Fall*. (Eddie Carbone in *A View from the Bridge* is another married man fascinated by a child-woman, but he is exonerated in another way: He is "sick.")

Miller expresses regret, in the Introduction to his *Collected Plays*, that he failed to make his villains sufficiently wicked; he thinks now that he should have represented them as being dedicated to evil for its own sake. I suspect that most students of *The Crucible* will feel that he has made them quite wicked enough. For one thing, he has established their depravity by inserting a number of clear references to the investigators and blacklisters of his own time. He has made Proctor ask, significantly: "Is the accuser always holy now?" To the automatic trustworthiness of accusers he has added the advantage of confession (always efficacious for former Communists), the necessity of naming the names of fellow-conspirators, the accusation of "an invisible crime" (witchcraft—or a crime of thought), the dangers threatening anyone who dares to defend the accused, the prejudice of the investigators, the absence of adequate legal defense for the accused, and the threat that those who protest will be charged with contempt of court. Most of these elements constitute what might be called a political case against the accusers and especially against the magistrates, Danforth and Hathorne. Miller builds an economic case as well, suggesting that the original adult instigators of the witchcraft trials were moved by greed, particularly by a desire for the victims' lands. The whole case is stated only in Miller's accompanying notes, but much of it is given dramatic form.

The viciousness of the children, except for Abigail, is less abundantly explained. We are evidently to assume that when they make their false charges they are breaking out of the restrictive forms of proper, pious, Puritan behavior to demand the attention that every child requires. The same rebelliousness has led them to dance in the moonlight and to join in Tituba's incantations. The discovery of these harmless occupations has led them to their more destructive

activity. Curiously, Miller chooses not to show us any good children
—a category to which the Proctors' offspring surely belong. We hear
of "Jonathan's trap" for rabbits, but these children are as absolutely
banished from the stage as the protagonists' children in Shaw's *Candida*. Most modern dramatists are less self-conscious about presenting children than Shaw was, but Miller makes a similar omission in *After the Fall*. At a climactic moment, Quentin is confronted with
his written statement that the only person in the world whom he
has ever loved is his daughter, and yet this child is never seen in
the play.

Over against the bad individual, the vengeful adults, and the
lying children, Miller sets the basically sound community, in which
the saintly Rebecca Nurse's benefactions are known even to the
stranger Hale. At best, Salem is a bad, quarrelsome place; the good
community is more warmly depicted in Miller's earlier plays, but
even in Salem it exists, and it furnishes twenty honest souls who will
not confess to witchcraft, even to save their lives. The underlying
presence of the good community, however misruled it may be, reminds us that Miller, even in face of his own evidence, professes to
believe in the basic strength and justice of the social organism, in
the possibility of good neighbors. If he criticizes society, he does so
from within, as a participant and a believer in it.

The deliberately antique language surely reflects Miller's self-consciousness regarding his emphatically heroic hero and the extreme situation in which he finds himself. Issues are never made so
clear, so black and white in any of Miller's other plays. And so,
naturally, the statement of these issues must be colored, must be, to
use Bertolt Brecht's term, "alienated" by quaint, unfamiliar ways of
speech. Certainly, the peculiar speech of *The Crucible* is not a
necessity, even in a play set in the seventeenth century. (Christopher
Fry's fifteenth-century Englishmen in *The Lady's Not for Burning*
speak a language closer to our own.) The purpose of the quirkish
English of *The Crucible* is not only to give the impression of an
antique time, although that is part of it; the purpose is to alienate
us, to make us unfamiliar in this setting, to permit distance to lend
its enchantment to this bare, simplistic confrontation of good and
evil, and also to keep us from making too immediate, too naive an
identification between these events and the parallel happenings of

our own time. The issues are too simple, much more simple than
the modern parallels. Language imposes a necessary complexity from
without.

Any final comment must dwell upon *The Crucible* as a play of
action and suspense. It falls short as a play of ideas, which is what it
was originally intended to be. It falls short because the parallels do
not fit and because Miller has had to adulterate—the pun is inten-
tional—Proctor's all too obvious innocence to create a specious kind
of guilt for him; he is easily exonerated of both crimes, the real one
and the unreal one, so easily that no ideas issue from the crucible of
this human destiny. And yet, *The Crucible* keeps our attention by
furnishing exciting crises, each one proceeding logically from its
predecessor, in the lives of people in whom we have been made to
take an interest. That is a worthy intention, if it is a modest one,
and it is suitably fulfilled.

The Crucible: A Structural View

by Philip G. Hill

The Crucible is too often spoken of as one of Arthur Miller's less successful plays. Its relative merits as compared with *Death of a Salesman* need not be argued here, but unquestionably the calumny that has been heaped upon it by well-meaning critics is little deserved—the play, however short it may fall of being *the* great American drama, is nevertheless a thoroughly successful, provocative, and stimulating theater piece. When competently performed, it can provide a deeply moving experience for the theatergoer.

The criticism of George Jean Nathan is perhaps typical. Nathan levels four principal charges at the play,[1] charges that in one form or another have been brought against it again and again by other critics. Nathan at least speaks from the advantageous position of having seen the play performed in New York, but too often it appears that wild charges are being flung at the play by critics who have never seen it staged—who have tried, perhaps inexpertly, to capture its full effectiveness from the printed page. This is a hazardous procedure at best, and in the case of *The Crucible* it has led to some gross distortions of what the play says and what it does. Let us examine each of Nathan's four charges and attempt to measure the validity of each.

In the first place, Nathan maintains that the power of the play is all "internal," that it is not communicated to an audience. If we take this criticism to imply that the action occurs within the mind and soul of the protagonist, then of course the statement that the

"The Crucible: *A Structural View*" by *Philip G. Hill. From* Modern Drama, *10 (December 1967), 312–17. Copyright © 1967; reprinted by permission of the University of Kansas.*

1. *The Theatre in the Fifties* (New York: Alfred A. Knopf, Inc., 1953), pp. 105–109.

play's power is internal is accurate, but that this in any sense damns the play is belied by the large number of plays throughout dramatic literature that have their action so centered and that are regarded as masterpieces. Most of the plays of Racine can be cited at once in support of this contention, together with selected plays of Euripides, Shakespeare, and Goethe, to name but a few. That *The Crucible* does not communicate this power to an audience is an allegation regarding which empirical evidence is lacking, but the long lines at the box offices of most theaters that have produced it since it "failed" on Broadway constitute, at least in part, a refutation of the charge. At one recent production of which the writer has first-hand knowledge, all previous attendance records were broken, and experienced theatergoers among the audience testified that they had enjoyed one of the rare and memorable theatrical experiences of their lives. This hardly describes a play that fails to communicate its power to the audience, whatever the quality of the production may have been.

The second charge brought by Nathan against *The Crucible,* and one that is almost universally pressed by those who are dissatisfied with the play, is that it suffers from poor character development. To this charge even the most vehement of its supporters must, in all justice, admit some truth. Elizabeth Proctor is a Puritan housewife, an honest woman, and a bit straight-laced; beyond this we know little of her. John Proctor is an upright and honest farmer confronted by a challenge to his honesty; more can and will be said of the struggles within his soul, but the fact remains that the multifaceted fascination of a Hamlet, an Oedipus, or even of a Willy Loman is indeed lacking. Danforth, on the other hand, is an all-too-recognizable human being: not at all the embodiment of all that is evil, but a conflicting mass of selfish motives and well-intentioned desires to maintain the status quo: not the devil incarnate, but a man convinced that a "good" end (maintaining the theocracy in colonial Massachusetts) can justify the most dubious means—in this case, the suborning of witnesses, the twisting of evidence, and the prostitution of justice. Reverend Hale, too, is a well-developed and many-faceted character, a man who arrives upon the scene confident of his power to exorcise the Devil in whatever form he may appear, and who by the end of the play can challenge every value for which a hero ever died: "Life is God's most precious gift; no principle, however glorious, may justify the taking of it."

Still, it must be admitted that the principal power of *The Crucible* does not lie in its character development. The characters are entirely adequate for the purposes for which Miller designed them, and no immutable law requires that every play depend upon characterization for its success, but certainly there is some justice in suggesting that *The Crucible* exhibits only a moderate degree of character development.

Nathan's next point of criticism is one that was heard from many of the New York critics at the time of the play's original production, but that has ceased to have much potency since the McCarthy era has passed into history. It was loudly proclaimed in 1953 that *The Crucible* was essentially propagandistic, that it struck too hard at an isolated phenomenon, and that thus it was at best a play of the immediate times and not for all time. The thirteen years that have passed since this charge was leveled, and the continued success of the play both in this country and abroad in the interim, drain from the assertion all of the efficacy that it may once have appeared to have. From the short view inescapably adopted by critics themselves caught up in the hysteria of McCarthyism, the play may well have seemed to push too hard the obvious parallels between witch-hunting in the Salem of 1692 and "witch-hunting" in the Washington and New York of 1952. If so, then we have simply one more reason to be grateful for the passing of this era, for unquestionably the play no longer depends upon such parallels. A whole generation of theatergoers has grown up in these intervening years to whom the name McCarthy is one vaguely remembered from newspaper accounts of the last decade, and who nevertheless find in *The Crucible* a powerful indictment of bigotry, narrow-mindedness, hypocrisy, and violation of due process of law, from whatever source these evils may spring. Unquestionably, if the play were tied inextricably to its alleged connection with a political phenomenon now buried (a connection that Miller denied all along), it would even today not have a very meaningful effect upon its audiences. And yet it does.

The fourth charge against the play, and the one brought by the more serious and insightful of the critics dealing with *The Crucible*, is at the same time the most challenging of the four. For Nathan, together with a host of other critics, attacks the basic structure of the play itself, claiming that it "draws up its big guns" too early in the play, and that by the end of the courtroom scene there is nowhere to go but down. This charge, indeed, gets at the very heart of the matter, and if it can be sustained it largely negates further argument regarding any relative merits that the play might exhibit. I submit, however, that the charge cannot be sustained—that, indeed, the critics adopting such an approach reveal a faulty knowledge of the play's structure and an inaccurate reading of its meaning. Indeed, Miller appears to me to have done a masterful job of sustaining a central action that by its very nature is "internal" and thus not conducive to easy dramatic development, and of sustaining this central action straight through to its logical conclusion at the end of the play.

The term "central action" is being used here in what I take to be its Aristotelian sense: one central objective that provides the play's plot structure with a beginning, a middle, and an end; when the objective is attained, the play is over. This central action may be described in the case of *The Crucible* as "to find John Proctor's soul," where the term "soul" is understood to mean Proctor's integrity, his sense of self-respect, what he himself variously calls his "honesty" and (finally) his "name." Proctor lost his soul, in this sense of the term, when he committed the crime of lechery with Abigail, and thus as the play opens there is wanted only a significant triggering incident to start Proctor actively on the search that will lead ultimately to his death. That this search for Proctor's soul will lead through the vagaries of a witch-hunt, a travesty of justice, and a clear choice between death and life without honor is simply the given circumstance of the play—no more germane to defining its central action than is the fact that Oedipus' search for the killer of Laius will lead through horror and incest to self-immolation. Thinking in these terms, then, it is possible to trace the development of this central action in a straightforward and rather elementary manner.

The structure of the play can conveniently be analyzed in terms of the familiar elements of the well-made play. The initial scenes involving Parris, Abigail, the Putnams, and the other girls serve quite satisfactorily the demands of simple exposition, and pave the way smoothly for the entrance of John Proctor. We learn quickly and yet naturally that a group of girls under Abby's leadership have conjured the Devil and that now at least two of them have experienced hysterical reactions that are being widely interpreted in terms of witchcraft. We also learn, upon Proctor's entrance, of the sexual attraction that still exists between him and Abby, and of the consummation of this attraction that has left John feeling that he has lost his soul. The inciting incident then occurs when Abby assures John that the girls' hysteria has "naught to do with witchcraft," a bit of knowledge that is very shortly to try John's honesty and lead him inevitably to his death.

The rising action of the play continues, then, through the arrival of Hale, Abby's denunciation of certain of the Puritan women (taking her cue from Tituba's success) in order to remove any taint of guilt from herself, and eventually, in the next scene, to the accusation of witchcraft being directed at Elizabeth Proctor. The significant point here, however, is that the rising action continues through the bulk of the courtroom scene, as horror piles upon horror, accusation upon accusation, and complication upon complication, until the action reaches not a climax but a *turning point* when Elizabeth, who purportedly cannot tell a lie, does lie in a misguided attempt to save her husband. This act on her part constitutes a turning point because, from that moment on, Proctor's doom is sealed; no device short of a totally unsatisfactory *deus ex machina* can save him from his inevitable fate. The *central action* of the play is not yet completed, however; Proctor has not yet found his soul, and even moderately skillful playing of the play's final scene can demonstrate quite clearly that this struggle goes on right up to the moment at which Proctor rips up his confession and chooses death rather than dishonor. Thus, this prison scene does not, as some critics have charged, constitute some sort of extended denouement that cannot possibly live up in intensity to the excitement of the courtroom scene, but rather the scene is, in technical terms, the *falling action* of the play, moving inevitably from the turning point to the climax.

This structural significance of the prison scene may be observed in a careful reading of the play, but it is more readily apparent in a competent production. Thus, it is the business of the actor playing Proctor to convey to the audience the fact that signing the confession and then refusing to hand it over to Danforth is not, as has so

often been charged, a delaying action and an anticlimactic complication on Miller's part, but rather a continuing and agonizing search
on Proctor's part for his honesty—for the course of action that will
be truest to his own honor and will recover for him his lost soul. In
a dilemma for which there is no simple solution, Proctor first sees
the efficacy of Hale's argument, that once life is gone there is no
further or higher meaning. Feeling that his honesty has long since
been compromised anyway, Proctor seriously feels a greater sense of
dishonor in appearing to "go like a saint," as Rebecca and the others
do, than in frankly facing up to his own dishonesty and saving his
life. On the strength of this argument, he signs the confession. Yet, as
Proctor stands there looking at his name on the paper (and here the
way in which the actor works with this property becomes all-impor-
tant), we have a visual, tangible stage metaphor for the struggle
that is going on within him. Proctor, unable fully to express the
significance of his own plight, cries out:

> Because it is my name! Because I cannot have another in my life!
> Because I lie and sign myself to lies! Because I am not worth the
> dust on the feet of them that hang! How may I live without my
> name? I have given you my soul; leave me my name!

The audience must see that this cry for his "name" is still the same
search that has been at the heart of the entire play, and that here it
has reached not some kind of anticlimax, but rather *the* climactic
moment of the play.

But in stating outright that his confession is a lie (and this is the
first moment at which he says so in so many words), Proctor triggers
in Danforth the one reaction that seals his own doom. For Danforth,
however narrow-minded and bigoted he may be, does indeed believe
in the fundamental fact of witchcraft, and he cannot allow a confession that is frankly and openly a lie:

> Is that document a lie? If it is a lie I will not accept it! What say
> you? I will not deal in lies, Mister! . . . You will give me your hon-
> est confession in my hand, or I cannot keep you from the rope. . . .
> What way do you go, Mister?

Thus stretched to the utmost on the rack of his dilemma, Proctor
makes the decision that costs him his life but restores to him his
soul: He tears up the confession. The denouement following this

climactic moment consumes not a whole scene as has frequently been charged, but a mere twelve lines. Proctor is led out to die, and Elizabeth speaks the epitaph that once again, finally, sums up the central action and significance of the play: "He have his goodness now. God forbid I take it from him!"

Thus, a close structural view of *The Crucible* reveals that this fourth charge against it is also an unfair and inaccurate one. The play, however it may appear in the reading, does not, in performance, rise to a climax in the courtroom scene that cannot be equalled. Certainly the tension of the courtroom scene is great; certainly the prison scene, if poorly performed, could be a letdown. But in a competent performance the inevitable movement from the turning point toward a climax, technically called the "falling action" but certainly involving no falling interest or intensity, continues through the prison scene to that moment at which Proctor rips up his confession, after which a quick denouement brings us to a satisfactory, and at the same time stunning, conclusion.

The play is certainly not one of the great plays of all time. Still, it has been maligned unduly by a series of critics who apparently were either too close to their critical trees to see the theatrical forest or were relying on an inadequate understanding of the play's structure. That this structure is not immediately apparent to the reader, but rather must be brought out in performance, may suggest some degree of weakness in Miller's dramaturgy, but is certainly not a damning weakness in itself. Plays are, after all, written to be performed on a stage, and the ultimate test of their success is their effectiveness under production conditions. *The Crucible* stands up very well to this test.

PART FOUR

Viewpoints

Jean-Paul Sartre's *Les Sorcières de Salem*

by Eric Mottram

. . . *Les Sorcières de Salem* (1957), a film made to Sartre's script by Raymond Rouleau, focuses clearly from its beginning on Proctor's rebellion against the use of personal power which condemns people as sinfully corrupt by inevitable theory. Proctor's sensuality and his identification of Elizabeth with the God of prohibiting sex and the God of judgment is firmly established, and Sartre enters into a general criticism of the Protestant ethic and its relations with sex, money and power relationships. The clerics link the devil with lower-class rebelliousness against the rich and powerful—in fact the storekeeper, from whom Elizabeth wishes to buy her daughter a doll, remarks: "There are no witches among the rich." Sin is overtly sin against state authority, only made to seem sin against Jonathan Edwards' God. In such a theocracy, the borderline beween actual "possession" and playacting is uncertain and some of the women in the meeting house climax are as "possessed" as the girls. An organization of "sensible citizens," both bourgeois and workers, sends a deputation to the Governor, but the lower classes come to distrust their leaders and plan among themselves to attack the gallows to forestall Proctor's execution. Danforth hopes to foil this plan by setting up the gallows inside the prison and welcomes the rebellion as an opportunity to strike at the people without remorseful conscience.

"Jean-Paul Sartre's Les Sorcières de Salem*" [editor's title] by Eric Mottram. From the chapter "Arthur Miller: The Development of a Political Dramatist in America," in John Russell Brown and Bernard Harris, eds.* American Theatre *(London: Edward Arnold Ltd., 1967), pp. 141–42. Copyright © 1967 by Edward Arnold Ltd. Reprinted by permission of the publisher.*

Sartre also has Abigail come to Proctor secretly, to make him confess so that they can escape to New York where no one will know of his shame; and she tempts him by threatening to become a whore in Boston. His desire for her cannot stand the idea of her body used by other men and he writes his confession accordingly. This has the effect, in the film, of making Abigail a far more sympathetic figure of passion, even when Proctor negotiates the crucial change from passion for her and love for Elizabeth. But he is hanged finally as pre-revolutionary martyr. Abigail's cries for help arouse the rebels to break into the prison but they would hang her too, as a traitor. As the final funeral cortege begins, it is Elizabeth who saves her: She quietly observes that she herself, and all of them, are guilty of the murder of Proctor. Her last words are: "Release her—she loved him," and Abigail stands shocked in a new understanding as the procession moves out of the village into the countryside.

Sartre has virtually filled out the sexual and historical details of Miller's play, which he treats as a sketch. But he also transforms Miller's characteristic despair and stress on a man's exemplary suicide into hope for social change through the murder of a hero. The film is more complex than the play, and more convincingly three-dimensional if rather more philosophically dogmatic. If the aim of such a historical drama is to analyse the present in order to change it, the deeper and wider the analysis the better. As Miller owned, *The Crucible* did not help to defeat McCarthy: "No liberal did that. The army defeated McCarthy. He attacked a general, and that was a deadly mistake" (*Guardian*, 23 January, 1965). The play's success came later, played to small non-commercial audiences already prepared to accept the liberalism it embodies. . . .

Action and Theme in *The Crucible*

by Robert Hogan

... *The Crucible* is a strong play, and its conclusion has much
of the force of tragedy. It has not the permeating compassion of
Death of a Salesman, but there is more dramatic power to John
Proctor's death than there was to Willy's. It is a harder-hitting play,
and its impact stems from Proctor's death being really a triumph.
You cannot pity a man who triumphs. Willy Loman's death was a
failure, and his suicide only a gesture of defeat. Him you can pity.

The Crucible is really a more dramatic play than *Death of a Salesman.* The earlier play attempted to construct a plot about Willy's
losing his job, and Biff's attempting to gain one, but these strands of
plot were only a frame on which to hang the exposition of a man's
whole life. The plots of *Death of a Salesman* are not the center of
the play, but in *The Crucible* the action is the play's very basis, its
consuming center. One watches *Death of a Salesman* to discover
what a man is like, but one watches *The Crucible* to discover what
a man does. *Death of a Salesman* is a tour de force that succeeds
despite its slim action because its real center is the accumulation of
enough significant detail to suggest a man. In the life of John Proctor, one single action is decisive, dominating, and totally pertinent,
and this action, this moment of decision and commitment, is that
climax toward which every incident in the play tends. *Death of a
Salesman* is not traditionally dramatic, at least in the Aristotelian
sense that the center of a drama is an action. *The Crucible* is so dramatic, and the centrality of its plot explains its greater strength.

That strength is also explained by the clarity with which the theme

"Action and Theme in The Crucible*"* [*editor's title*]. *From Robert Hogan,
Arthur Miller* (*Minneapolis: University of Minnesota Press, American Writers
Series, 1964*), *pp. 27-29. Copyright © 1964 by the University of Minnesota. Re-
printed by permission of the publisher.*

of *The Crucible* emerges from its plot. The theme of *Death of a Salesman* does not emerge so much from its story as from its illustration and exposition. For that reason it is necessary for Linda and Charley in their laments to explain the meaning of Willy's life, and actually Linda is still explaining what the play means in the last scene. *The Crucible* requires no such exposition, for the play's meaning has been acutely dramatized. The exposition in *Death of a Salesman* is dramatic only in the way that the keening in *Riders to the Sea* is dramatic. It is a lyrical evocation of emotion rather than a dramatic one.

The Crucible is more traditionally dramatic in one other way. The theme of a play is made more intense by the hero's either making a discovery of past folly (Oedipus, Lear) or being presented with an agonizing dilemma (Orestes, Hamlet). Proctor's story has elements of both situations. His past folly, which he has been trying unsuccessfully to live down, is his seduction of Abigail Williams, and this fault eventually destroys him when Abigail turns against him and accuses him of witchcraft. The center of the play, however, is his dilemma about commitment. This dilemma is stated in each act in somewhat different terms. In Act I, Proctor washes his hands of the town's problem and refuses to be involved in the absurd charges of witchcraft being made by a small group of frightened, hysterical girls. In Act II, he is pushed into involvement when Abigail denounces his wife Elizabeth as a witch. In Act III, he attempts legally to rescue the accused, but by resorting to law also attempts to avoid being involved himself. Finally, at the end of the act, he can only achieve justice by involvement, and so he accuses Abigail and becomes himself one of the accused. Proctor's identification with the accused is not yet total. He drags his feet as did Lawrence Newman. He suffers with them for months in prison, but in the final moment before his execution he signs a confession of witchcraft. His reason is that he is really different from them. He cries: "I cannot mount the gibbet like a saint. It is a fraud. I am not that man. My honesty is broke, Elizabeth; I am no good man. Nothing's spoiled by giving them this lie that were not rotten long before." Proctor is still striving for a compromise, but Miller will allow him none. Proctor signs the confession to save his life, but the judges demand that the confession be made public, and he finds that he cannot live in society uncommitted. He must be either totally and publicly against the accused or totally and publicly with them. There is no middle ground of private commitment and public neutrality. This is Proctor's final dilemma as it was Lawrence Newman's and Joe Keller's, and Miller will not, at this point in his career, allow the individual to escape from his social obligation into his private life.

Arthur Miller and the Idea of
Modern Tragedy

by M. W. Steinberg

. . . The same dichotomy persists in *The Crucible* between the concept of tragedy evidenced in the problem play, with the focus of interest on social conditions that are expressed through characters and their interactions, and the pre-modern, or what has been called the Christian tragedy, in which the focus of attention is on the tragic hero and the social context is given what significance it has through its bearing on him. Though *The Crucible* is a very powerful drama, structurally it suffers from Miller's failure to resolve this confusion. The introduction which outlines the social context, the opening scene, and large sections of the play later provide more than a background before which the protagonist acts. They have a significance greater than necessary for the playing out of the tragedy of John Proctor. The diffusion of the tragic force that results from the dramatist presenting the evil in society crushing Giles Corey, Rebecca Nurse, and others, as well as John Proctor, supports this view. Miller is clearly interested in showing the larger social effects of the particular blight that concerns him here. Even though we can agree with him that *The Crucible* is not merely a response to McCarthyism, or an attempt to cure witch-hunting, any more than the intention of *Death of a Salesman* is to improve conditions for travellers, nevertheless the concern with the political problem was obvious when the play appeared in 1953. Indeed Miller, in an article on *The Crucible*, reiterates his earlier statement that the dramatist cannot consider man apart from his social con-

Excerpted from "Arthur Miller and the Idea of Modern Tragedy" by M. W. Steinberg. From The Dalhousie Review, *40 (1960), 329-40. Copyright © 1960; reprinted by permission of Dalhousie University.*

text and the problems that his environment presents. "I believe," he writes, "that it is no longer possible to contain the truth of the human situation so totally within a single man's guts as the bulk of our plays presuppose." It is not merely that man and the environment interact, but that they are part of each other—"The fish is in the water and the water is in the fish." We in the twentieth century, Miller adds, are more aware than any preceding generation "of the larger units that help make us and destroy us. . . . The vast majority of us know now—not merely as knowledge but as feeling, feeling capable of expression in art—that we are being formed, that our alternatives in life are not absolutely our own, as the romantic play inevitably must presuppose." Then, with specific reference to *The Crucible,* he says further, "The form, the shape, the meaning of *The Crucible* were all compounded out of the faith of those who were hanged. They were asked to be lonely and they refused. . . . It was not good to cast this play, to form it so that the psyche of the hero should emerge so 'commonly' as to wipe out of mind the process itself, the spectacle of that faith. . . ."

And yet the play, after the opening scene, becomes increasingly concerned with the role of one man, John Proctor, and the crisis that is inner, though prompted by outside forces. The intensity of the tragedy results from this increasing concentration on the individual, the tragic hero, who, in his dilemma, epitomizes the whole tragic situation. Whether Miller intended it or not, the play compels us to focus on Proctor (unfortunately not always), and through him we realize most clearly Miller's theme, which, as he also tells us, is "the conflict between a man's raw deeds and his conception of himself; the question of whether conscience is in fact an organic part of the human being, and what happens when it is handed over not merely to the state or the mores of the time but to one's friend or wife. The big difference, I think, is that *The Crucible* sought to include a higher degree of consciousness than the earlier plays." This higher degree of consciousness is very important, as it raises the stature of the hero, makes him a worthier protagonist, and renders more significant the role of will. Only if the hero knows the issue and sees clearly his position can his struggle become a clear expression of will and character. Only when the will is conscious can it be heroic and the protagonist become more than a victim like Willy

Loman, whose will to resist degrading conditions is really nullified by his acceptance of them—an acceptance made possible by his very limited vision.

Though *The Crucible* was undoubtedly prompted in part by a contemporary political situation for which the Salem witch-hunt was an apt counterpart, and though Miller may well have intended to write a tragic problem play, he seems to have become increasingly concerned with and even carried away by the tragedy in individual human terms. Indeed in the Introduction to his *Collected Plays* Miller tells us that it was an individual's crisis, not a social issue, that precipitated the play:

> I doubt that I should ever have tempted agony by actually writing a play on the subject [the Salem witch-hunt] had I not come upon a single fact. It was that Abigail Williams, the prime mover of the Salem hysteria, so far as the hysterical children were concerned, had a short time earlier been the house servant of the Proctors and now was crying out Elizabeth Proctor as a witch; but more—it was clear from the record that with entirely uncharacteristic fastidiousness she was refusing to include John Proctor, Elizabeth's husband, in her accusations despite the urgings of the prosecutors.

Which Witch Is Which?

by James W. Douglass

. . . The comment made by *The Crucible* on the existence of
witches is that their only mode of existence is in the mind of the
accuser, at least until the accused has surrendered himself to that
mind. When he does make the surrender, the accused consents to his
being absorbed into the other's accusation, and with the loss of his
own identity becomes truly the content of that accusation, a witch
himself. The loss of personal integrity, of the individual's resistance
to outside manipulations, makes him pliable to the demands of the
witch-hunter. As an individual he becomes nothing more than an
objective correlative, a spatially distinct form of the idea held
securely in the accuser's consciousness. As long as he maintains the
uniqueness of his own beliefs, making no surrender, the individual
will be able to recognize himself. But if he surrenders those beliefs,
or as Mr. Miller puts it, if he "hands over his conscience to another,"
he will become whatever that ruling consciousness wishes him to be,
be, its now subservient witch.

Even if Proctor signed a confession while withholding his internal consent, he would still, in the context of *The Crucible,* become a witch. The "witch" by accusation only, would, by his act of
signing and in spite of his inner reservations, admit in the very
depths of his soul the truth of the court's charge. For what in the
prosecution's terms is a witch but one who consorts with the Devil?
And who in Mr. Miller's term is the Devil but the prosecution itself? By signing his name to a confession dictated by the court,
John Proctor would in fact be signing the Book of the Devil, for

Excerpted from "Miller's The Crucible: *Which Witch Is Which?" by James W.
Douglass. From* Renascence, *15 (Spring 1963), 145–51. Copyright © 1963; reprinted by permission of the publisher and the author.*

Mr. Miller has made it clear that the real Devil in *The Crucible* is that same faction which nominally seeks the Devil's defeat.

In a drama filled with ironies, the biggest irony is that its author seems wholly unconscious of the fact that a Devil, even a Devil of his own creation, is actually present in *The Crucible*. Both in his play and in a long introduction to his *Collected Plays* published in 1957, Mr. Miller has given us a number of remarks on the problem of evil and the Devil. In a narrative portion of *The Crucible* available only to his reading audience, the playwright makes clear his own metaphysics of good and evil:

> Since 1692 a great but superficial change has wiped out God's beard and the Devil's horns, but the world is still gripped between two diametrically opposed absolutes. The concept of unity, in which positive and negative are attributes of the same force, in which good and evil are relative, ever-changing, and always joined to the same phenomenon—such a concept is still reserved to the physical sciences and to the few who have grasped the history of ideas. . . . When we see the steady and methodical inculcation into humanity of the idea of man's worthlessness—until redeemed—the necessity of the Devil may become evident as a weapon, a weapon designed and used time and time again in every age to whip men into a surrender to a particular church or church-state. . . . A political policy is equated with moral right, and opposition to it with diabolical malevolence.

The Devil is only an ideological weapon. Evil can never be absolute, but only relative, ever-changing. In a later essay the holder of these views defends himself against the critics who "have taken exception . . . to the unrelieved badness of the prosecution in my play" by claiming:

> I was up against historical facts which were immutable. . . . I do not think that either the record itself or the numerous commentaries upon it reveal any mitigation of the unrelieved, straightforward, and absolute dedication to evil displayed by the judges of these trials and the prosecutors. . . . I sought but could not at the time take hold of a concept of man which might really begin to account for such evil.

Although he rejects the idea of an "absolute" in referring to the forces of good and evil, and indeed blames an adherence to absolutes for the persecutions of history, Mr. Miller finds it necessary to return to the term in defending his own portrayal of the evil prosecution. By his larger frame of reference, these men are "absolutely dedicated" to a reality that is itself relative and ever-changing, existing in a kind of polarity with good. Such a reality does not seem to explain the violent depths of evil which Mr. Miller claims to have found in Salem, and which we find in *The Crucible.* The playwright himself is troubled in the above quotation by this disparity between his metaphysics and his drama. Nor does the explanation seem to lie in man alone, because Mr. Miller admits that he could take hold of no concept of man "which might really begin to account for such evil."

Whether or not we see a theology of absolutes as the only satisfying explanation for the evil shown in the prosecution, we can convict Mr. Miller on his own terms of including the Devil in his cast. The Devil, according to the playwright's view of history, arrives on the scene when "a political policy is equated with moral right, and opposition to it with diabolical malevolence." But if we reverse the usual sin of orthodoxy, which attributes diabolical malevolence to the government's opposition, and instead attribute diabolical malevolence to the government, how far have we traveled from the original "Devil-error"? We have only returned to the Devil in a different form. Unrelieved evil, regardless of whether we signify it by the term "absolute," is as much an attribute of the prosecution in Mr. Miller's eyes, as he would have us think it was an attribute of the accused in the prosecution's eyes. *The Crucible* tells us not that there were no witches in Salem, but that the witches were all members of the prosecution. Instead of a pin-pricked doll, the Devil had a gavel in his hand. . . .

Subjectivism and Self-Awareness

by Sheila Huftel

. . . Because of Miller's driving need to know *why*—his first and
last question—the way people think is as important to him as the
way they feel. It is this that dictates his move away from subjectivism
to greater self-awareness in *The Crucible*. The flaw complained of
in Willy Loman was corrected in John Proctor, and, for many reasons, prompted greater dissatisfaction. As Miller points out, audiences and critics alike are conditioned to subjectivism and for this
reason found more common ground with Willy, regardless of the
period of the play. The character was altogether more graspable
to them. An audience will more readily accept a character governed
by feeling, like Willy Loman, than one who cannot help thinking
aloud, attracted to analysis, like John Proctor or Quentin. Their
awareness seems to make them at once remote and detached. Audiences, for the present, tend to walk away from it, primarily because
they are less interested in knowing *why* than is Arthur Miller.

Where Miller is interested in causes, the audience cares only for
results. Rightly, Miller presupposes: "But certainly the passion of
knowing is as powerful as the passion of feeling alone." Only to
find that there is nothing certain about it. His passion for awareness is not new. Shaw had it, so did Brecht. What *is* new is Miller's
insistence that subjectivism's higher stage is not self-awareness, but
a synthesis of feeling and awareness.

In *The Crucible* the synthesis Miller has in mind lies more in
the play as a whole than in his characters. It is not achieved in a
single character until Quentin in *After the Fall*. *The Crucible*
counteracts etched characters with a text full to overflowing with

"Subjectivism and Self-Awareness" [*editor's title*]. *From Sheila Huftel*, Arthur
Miller: The Burning Glass (*New York: Citadel Press, 1965*), *pp. 142–44. Copyright © 1965 by Citadel Press, Inc. Reprinted by permission of the publisher.*

passion. The play is written in a powerful, mounting prose, and the height and pitch of the dramatic scenes are found nowhere else in Miller's work. This particular balance held between play and character is necessary. Without it and with more subjective character-drawing the play could easily collapse into chaos. The second problem solved by this balance is that of "remoteness" in an aware character who, from the audience's point of view, thinks too much. Spare character-drawing is not new for Miller; with his minor characters he has always told you precisely what you need to know of them and nothing more. Here the technique extends from Giles and Rebecca to John and Elizabeth. But this leanness does not make the agony of John Proctor's outbursts any less real. A character does not become unreal because he speaks only those lines that will define him. To assume that he does is to confuse realism with naturalism. The width between the two is no more than a razor's edge, but the difference is basic.

Fortunately, this argument does not stop at theory. We do not need to guess at what *The Crucible* would become with more subjective characters. Sartre's film, a very free version of the play, proves Miller's argument. John Proctor did not become more "real" by being played as a guilt-torn neurotic. He did not have more feeling, but simply the wrong kind. I watched unmoved while Yves Montand twitched in time to his tormented soul, and came out murmuring that Miller would never have created such a character. Miller's John Proctor would fight the final holocaust. The earth could split and rocks could fall like hail, and still he would be there. When Proctor finds he can face hanging, he is discovering again, as have Miller's other heroes before him, what a man can do and how much he can support to keep his own integrity.

Basically the same idea drives both Proctor and Willy Loman, in that neither can break away from the unspoken demand behind the play. And again the belief is Miller's refusal to understand or accept passivity or placidity. When he was in London at a symposium arranged by *Encore,* he protested: "I don't understand why anything has to be accepted. I don't get it." The easygoing English found this laughable. They seemed a little embarrassed by all this high earnestness when everybody else had been playing at debate. Nothing half as serious had been thought on that panel, far less said. This rejection of compliance is fundamental in Miller; that once grasped, laughter changes to alarm. It is the attitude of a man who would smilingly send you out to change the world.

At a performance of the play in Bristol the atmosphere was so faithfully created that the audience reacted as if somebody had thrown a firecracker into the auditorium. If they could, they would have pushed back their chairs. One fragile old lady looked around the delicate eighteenth-century theatre as if in fear for its survival. . . .

The Silence of Arthur Miller

by Arthur Ganz

. . . The pattern of strength through self-knowledge, though apparent in *All My Sons,* is somewhat obscured by the suggestion that the central character is merely a victim of social forces and, therefore, not entirely responsible for his actions. In Miller's early novel, *Focus,* and in his play, *The Crucible,* however, the pattern stands out clearly, though these works are even more obviously social studies than *All My Sons.* But the enemy that Miller chooses to fight in each of these two works is so clearly an evil, as it is not in *All My Sons* and *Death of a Salesman,* that when the hero finally summons up strength to combat it, his virtue need not be questioned. . . .

. . . In finding his own identity, Proctor, like Lawrence Newman [in *Focus*], finds the strength to do battle with the enemy. Exactly who that enemy is Miller has not made clear, for despite his later protestations that the Salem judges are consciously evil, we do not know from the text whether they are sincere but narrow believers in the supernatural, authoritarians who find witchcraft a convenient instrument for repression, or merely sadists. Miller has been so careful to keep his parable from being limited by the special circumstances of the McCarthy era that he has perhaps prevented it from being very like the circumstances of any era. But however vague Miller may be in depicting the exact nature of villainy, he is precise in showing the nature of heroism. As always with Miller, it lies in self-knowledge.

In the simple worlds of *Focus* and *The Crucible,* where the good are very good and the bad are monsters, heroism is a comparatively

Excerpted from "The Silence of Arthur Miller" by Arthur Ganz. From Drama Survey, *3 (1963), 224–37. Copyright © 1963; reprinted by permission of the University of Minnesota and the author.*

easy matter. (Thus it is not surprising that Miller was attracted to one of Ibsen's least complicated plays, *An Enemy of the People,* nor that in his adaptation he has further simplified it, converting the irascible, bumbling, half-comic Dr. Stockman into a man of clear and noble character, a paragon of the social virtues.) But when one turns from social morality and enters the heroic world of classical tragedy [in *A View from the Bridge*], a belief in an automatic virtue attending on self-knowledge is not so easy to maintain. That Miller should choose to enter this world after dealing directly or symbolically with social themes in all his previous plays is significant, for it suggests a discontent with these themes or with his ability to handle them. That he should remain silent for eight years after his one essay in this genre suggests the existence of an even deeper discontent, one that may perhaps stem from Miller's recognition of the limitation of the pattern of virtue through self-knowledge, which has persisted even here amid the appurtenances of tragedy imported to Brooklyn.

PART FIVE

Additional Scene

A Private Meeting of John and Abigail

by Arthur Miller

Scene. A wood. Night.
Proctor appears with lantern. He enters glancing behind him, then halts, holding the lantern raised. Abigail appears with a wrap over her nightgown, her hair down. A moment of questioning silence.
Proctor [*searching*]. I must speak with you, Abigail. *She does not move, staring at him.* Will you sit?
Abigail. How do you come?
Proctor. Friendly.
Abigail [*glancing about*]. I don't like the woods at night. Pray you, stand closer. *He comes closer to her, but keeps separated in spirit.* I knew it must be you. When I heard the pebbles on the window, before I opened up my eyes I knew. I thought you would come a good time sooner.
Proctor. I had thought to come many times.
Abigail. Why didn't you? I am so alone in the world now.
Proctor [*as a fact. Not bitterly*]. Are you? I've heard that people come a hundred mile to see your face these days.
Abigail. Aye, my face. Can you see my face?
Proctor [*holds the lantern to her face*]. Then you're troubled?
Abigail. Have you come to mock me?
Proctor [*sets lantern and sits down*]. No, no, but I hear only that you go to the tavern every night, and play shovelboard with the Deputy Governor, and they give you cider.
Abigail [*as though that did not count*]. I have once or twice played the shovelboard. But I have no joy in it.

"A Private Meeting of John and Abigail" [*editor's title*]. *From Arthur Miller, The Crucible (New York: The Viking Press, Inc., 1953). Copyright 1953 by Arthur Miller. Reprinted by permission of the Viking Press, Inc., and The International Famous Agency. This scene was added to Act II in a revised version of the play first produced in New York in July, 1953.*

Proctor [*he is probing her*]. This is a surprise, Abby. I'd thought to find you gayer than this. I'm told a troop of boys go step for step with you wherever you walk these days.

Abigail. Aye, they do. But I have only lewd looks from the boys.

Proctor. And you like that not?

Abigail. I cannot bear lewd looks no more, John. My spirit's changed entirely. I ought to be given Godly looks when I suffer for them as I do.

Proctor. Oh? How do you suffer, Abby?

Abigail [*pulls up dress*]. Why, look at my leg. I'm holes all over from their damned needles and pins. *Touching her stomach.* The jab your wife gave me's not healed yet, y'know.

Proctor [*seeing her madness now*]. Oh, it isn't.

Abigail. I think sometimes she pricks it open again while I sleep.

Proctor. Ah?

Abigail. And George Jacobs . . . *Sliding up her sleeve.* He comes again and again and raps me with his stick—the same spot every night all this week. Look at the lump I have.

Proctor. Abby—George Jacobs is in the jail all this month.

Abigail. Thank God he is, and bless the day he hangs and lets me sleep in peace again! Oh, John, the world's so full of hypocrites. *Astonished, outraged.* They pray in jail! I'm told they all pray in jail!

Proctor. They may not pray?

Abigail. And torture me in my bed while sacred words are comin' from their mouths? Oh, it will need God himself to cleanse this town properly!

Proctor. Abby—you mean to cry out still others?

Abigail. If I live, if I am not murdered, I surely will, until the last hypocrite is dead.

Proctor. Then there is no one good?

Abigail [*softly*]. Aye, there is one. *You* are good.

Proctor. Am I? How am I good?

Abigail. Why, you taught me goodness, therefore you are good. It were a fire you walked me through, and all my ignorance was burned away. It were a fire, John, we lay in fire. And from that night no woman dare call me wicked anymore but I knew my answer. I used to weep for my sins when the wind lifted up my skirts; and blushed for shame because some old Rebecca called me loose. And then you burned my ignorance away. As bare as some December tree I saw them all—walking like saints to church, running to feed the sick, and hypocrites in their hearts! And God gave me strength to call them liars, and God made men to listen to me, and by God I will scrub the world clean for the love of Him! Oh, John, I will make you such a wife when the world is white again! *She kisses his hand in high emotion.* You will be amazed to see me every day, a light of heaven in your house, a . . . *He rises and backs away, frightened, amazed.* Why are you cold?

Proctor [*in a business-like way, but with uneasiness, as though before an unearthly thing*]. My wife goes to trial in the morning, Abigail.

Abigail [*distantly*]. Your wife?

Proctor. Surely you knew of it?

Abigail [*coming awake to that*]. I do remember it now. *As a duty.* How —how—is she well?

Proctor. As well as she may be, thirty-six days in that place.

Abigail. You said you came friendly.

Proctor. She will not be condemned, Abby.

Abigail [*her holy feelings outraged. But she is questioning*]. You brought me from my bed to speak of her?

Proctor. I come to tell you, Abby, what I will do tomorrow in the court. I would not take you by surprise, but give you all good time to think on what to do to save yourself.

Abigail [*incredibly, and with beginning fear*]. Save myself!

Proctor. If you do not free my wife tomorrow, I am set and bound to ruin you, Abby.

Abigail [*her voice small—astonished*]. How—ruin me?

Proctor. I have rocky proof in documents that you knew that poppet were none of my wife's; and that you yourself bade Mary Warren stab that needle into it.

Abigail [*a wildness stirs in her; a child is standing here who is unutterably frustrated, denied her wish; but she is still grasping for her wits*]. I bade Mary Warren . . . ?

Proctor. You know what you do, you are not so mad!

Abigail [*she calls upwards*]. Oh, hypocrites! Have you won him, too? *Directly to him.* John, why do you let them send you?

Proctor. I warn you, Abby.

Abigail. They send you! They steal your honesty and . . .

Proctor. I have found my honesty.

Abigail. No, this is your wife pleading, your sniveling, envious wife! This is Rebecca's voice, Martha Corey's voice. You were no hypocrite!

Proctor [*he grasps her arm and holds her*]. I will prove you for the fraud you are!

Abigail. And if they ask you why Abigail would ever do so murderous a deed, what will you tell them?

Proctor [*it is hard even to say it*]. I will tell them why.

Abigail. What will you tell? You will confess to fornication? In the court?

Proctor. If you will have it so, so I will tell it! *She utters a disbelieving laugh. I say I will! *She laughs louder, now with more assurance he will never do it. He shakes her roughly.* If you can still hear, hear this! Can you hear! *She is trembling, staring up at him as though he were out of his mind.* You will tell the court you are blind to spirits; you cannot see them anymore, and you will never cry witchery again, or I will make you famous for the whore you are!

Abigail [*she grabs him*]. Never in this world! I know you, John—you are this moment singing secret Hallelujahs that your wife will hang!

Proctor [*throws her down*]. You mad, you murderous bitch!

Abigail [*rises*]. Oh, how hard it is when pretense falls! But it falls, it falls! *She wraps herself up as though to go.* You have done your duty by her. I hope it is your last hypocrisy. I pray you will come again with sweeter news for me. I know you will—now that your duty's done. Good night, John. *She is backing away, raising her hand in farewell.* Fear naught. I will save you tomorrow. From yourself I will save you. *She is gone.*

Proctor is left alone, amazed in terror. He takes up his lantern and slowly exits as

THE CURTAIN FALLS

Chronology of Important Dates

	Arthur Miller	The Age
1915	Born in Harlem, New York City.	Edgar Lee Masters, *Spoon River Anthology*.
1917		U.S. declares war against Germany. T. S. Eliot, *Prufrock and Other Observations*.
1919		Eighteenth (Prohibition) Amendment enacted. Sherwood Anderson, *Winesburg, Ohio*.
1920		Sinclair Lewis, *Main Street;* Eugene O'Neill, *The Emperor Jones*.
1922		Eliot, *The Waste Land;* O'Neill, *The Hairy Ape*.
1924		O'Neill, *Desire Under the Elms*.
1925		Scopes "Monkey" trial. Theodore Dreiser, *An American Tragedy;* F. Scott Fitzgerald, *The Great Gatsby;* Ezra Pound, *Cantos*.
1926		Ernest Hemingway, *The Sun Also Rises*.

113

1929	In financial straits, family moves to Brooklyn.	Depression begins with stock market collapse. William Faulkner, *The Sound and the Fury;* Thomas Wolfe, *Look Homeward, Angel;* Hemingway, *A Farewell to Arms.*
1932–1934	Graduates from high school. Works as clerk in automobile parts warehouse.	
1934	Admitted to University of Michigan.	Lillian Hellman, *The Little Foxes;* O'Neill, *Ah, Wilderness.*
1936	First play, *Honors at Dawn,* produced at the university; awarded Avery Hopwood prize.	Nobel Prize to O'Neill. Clifford Odets, *Paradise Lost.*
1937	*No Villain* produced at the university.	Odets, *Golden Boy.*
1938	*They Too Arise,* a revision of *No Villain,* receives Theatre Guild and Hopwood Awards. Graduates. Joins Federal Theatre Project in New York.	Thornton Wilder, *Our Town.*
1938–1943	Writes plays for Project and for radio. Marries Mary Grace Flattery; holds variety of jobs to support young family.	William Saroyan, *The Time of Your Life* (1939), *Love's Old Sweet Song* (1940).
1939		World War II begins. John Steinbeck, *The Grapes of Wrath.*
1941		December 7: Attack on Pearl Harbor brings U.S. into World War II.

1942		Wilder, *The Skin of Our Teeth.*
1944	*Situation Normal,* journal of Army camp tour, published. *The Man Who Had All the Luck* produced, awarded Theatre Guild National prize, and published (Miller's first play on Broadway).	
1945	*Focus,* a novel, published.	Nuclear destruction of two Japanese cities brings World War II to end. Richard Wright, *Black Boy;* Tennessee Williams, *The Glass Menagerie.*
1947	*All My Sons* produced and published; receives New York Drama Critics' Circle Award.	O'Neill, *A Moon for the Misbegotten.*
1948	*All My Sons* produced as film.	Williams, *A Streetcar Named Desire, Summer and Smoke;* Norman Mailer, *The Naked and the Dead.*
1949	*Death of a Salesman* produced and published; receives Pulitzer Prize, among other awards.	
1950	*An Enemy of the People,* adaptation of Ibsen's play, produced and published.	Alger Hiss convicted of perjury concerning alleged espionage activities in 1930s. Korean War begins. Nobel Prize to Faulkner.
1951	*Death of a Salesman* produced as film.	

1953	*The Crucible* produced and published; awarded Antoinette Perry Prize.	Korean Armistice. William Inge, *Picnic.*
1954	State Department denies Miller a passport to attend Brussels première of *The Crucible.*	Army-McCarthy hearings. Supreme Court bans segregation in public schools. McCarthy censured by Senate. Nobel Prize to Hemingway. Williams, *Cat on a Hot Tin Roof.*
1955	*A View from the Bridge* and *A Memory of Two Mondays* produced and published. Miller's political beliefs investigated by New York City Youth Board. Divorces wife.	
1956	Questioned by House Committee on Un-American Activities; refuses to name suspected Communist sympathizers. Awarded honorary doctorate by University of Michigan. Marries Marilyn Monroe. An expanded *View from the Bridge* produced in London.	O'Neill, *Long Day's Journey Into Night.*
1957	*Collected Plays* published. French version of *The Crucible* filmed. Convicted for contempt of Congress (decision later reversed).	Inge, *The Dark at the Top of the Stairs.*
1958	Elected to National Institute of Arts and Letters.	
1959	Wins Institute's Gold Medal for Drama.	

1961–1962	Film of *The Misfits* produced and screen play published. Divorces Marilyn Monroe.	
1962	*A View from the Bridge* produced as film. Marries Inge Morath.	U.S.-Russian nuclear confrontation over Cuba. First orbital space flight. Nobel Prize to Steinbeck. Edward Albee, *Who's Afraid of Virginia Woolf?*
1963		President Kennedy assassinated.
1964	*After the Fall* and *Incident at Vichy* produced.	
1965	Elected President of P.E.N. (international association of Poets, Essayists, and Novelists). *Incident at Vichy* published.	Civil Rights Act. President Johnson intervenes in Santo Domingo and escalates war in South Vietnam.
1967	*I Don't Need You Any More,* a short-story collection, published. *The Crucible* produced on television.	
1968	*The Price* produced and published.	Martin Luther King, Jr., and Robert F. Kennedy assassinated.
1969	"In Russia," an essay, with photographs by Inge Morath, published.	First manned flight to moon.
1970		U.S. and South Vietnamese troops enter Cambodia.
1972	*The Creation of the World and Other Business* scheduled for fall production.	

Notes on the Editor and Contributors

JOHN FERRES, the editor of this volume, teaches in the Department of American Thought and Language at Michigan State University. He has written on Sherwood Anderson and British Commonwealth authors, edited Anderson's *Winesburg, Ohio* (for the Viking Critical Library) and *Many Marriages,* and is currently co-editing a volume of criticism on British Commonwealth literature.

HERBERT BLAU is Academic Vice-President and Dean of the Theatre School at California Institute of the Arts. He was a co-director of the San Francisco Actor's Workshop and, later, of the Repertory Theatre of Lincoln Center in New York. In addition to his *The Impossible Theatre,* he is the author of two plays and many articles on theatre and the arts.

PENELOPE CURTIS teaches English at the University of Melbourne, Australia. Interested in medieval literature and drama, she has published essays on Chaucer and Anton Chekhov and is presently completing a book on *The Canterbury Tales.*

JAMES W. DOUGLASS is a Catholic writer and thinker. Formerly a consultant to the second Vatican Council, his book, *The Non-Violent Cross: a Theology of Revolution and Peace,* examines the role of the ecumenical church as a mediating force for peace and reform.

ARTHUR GANZ is Associate Professor of English at the City College of The City University of New York. He is the editor of the Twentieth Century Views volume on Harold Pinter and the author of numerous articles on playwrights such as Oscar Wilde, Anton Chekhov, Jean Giraudoux, and Tennessee Williams.

JOHN GASSNER, now dead, was Sterling Professor of Playwriting and Dramatic Literature at Yale University and, previously, head of the Play Department of the Theatre Guild in New York. Among his many important books on the drama are *Masters of the Drama, Form and Idea in the Modern Theatre,* and *Theatre at the Crossroads.*

118

RICHARD HAYES was drama critic of *Commonweal* in the 1950s. He is the editor of *Port Royal and Other Plays,* an anthology of modern French plays in translation.

PHILIP G. HILL is Chairman of the Department of Drama and Speech at Furman University. As with the piece on *The Crucible,* his essays on drama often grow out of personal experience and insight gained by directing productions of plays.

ROBERT HOGAN teaches English at the University of California at Davis. Besides his *Arthur Miller,* he is the author or editor of numerous books on Anglo-Irish literature and modern drama and is a playwright as well.

SHEILA HUFTEL is a British journalist and critic. She is the author of *Arthur Miller: The Burning Glass.*

WALTER KERR may be considered the dean of American drama critics. Since 1966 he has been the Sunday drama critic of *The New York Times,* having served in a similar capacity on *The New York Herald Tribune* and *Commonweal.* His work received the George Jean Nathan Award for Dramatic Criticism in 1964. He is the author of eight books on the theatre.

GEORGE LYMAN KITTREDGE, who died in 1941, enjoyed an illustrious career as philologist and professor of English at Harvard University. In his day he was the most influential American teacher and writer on Shakespearean and earlier English literature. Two of his monuments are his editions of Shakespeare's complete works and twenty-nine volumes of English Classics in the Athenaeum Press series.

EARL LATHAM is Joseph B. Eastman Professor of Political Science and Chairman of the department at Amherst College. Among the eighteen books he has written, edited, or contributed to are *The Group Basis of Politics* and *The Communist Controversy in Washington,* a prize-winning study of the Truman years.

LEONARD MOSS is Director of Comparative Literature at the State University College at Geneseo, New York. He has published many articles on the theory and practice of tragedy in addition to his book on Arthur Miller.

ERIC MOTTRAM lectures in American Literature and American Studies at the University of London and was recently Visiting Professor at Kent State University. He has published and edited books on William Faulkner, William Burroughs, and Kenneth Rexroth; co-edited *The Penguin Companion to American Literature;* and written two volumes of poetry. He is the editor of *Poetry Review.*

EDWARD MURRAY is Associate Professor of English at the State University of New York at Brockport. His forthcoming *The Cinematic Imagination* follows books on Miller and Clifford Odets.

HENRY POPKIN is Professor of English at the State University of New York at Buffalo and has written extensively on the modern drama for periodicals (*Partisan Review, Kenyon Review, Mademoiselle, Vogue*) and newspapers (*The New York Times,* London *Times*). He is the editor of *Modern British Drama* and *The Concise Encyclopedia of Modern Drama,* as well as several plays in the Avon Books series.

M. W. STEINBERG teaches English at the University of British Columbia. He is the author of numerous articles on Canadian writers, co-author of *Discipline and Discovery,* and editor of *Aspects of Modern Drama.* In 1956 he initiated and organized the first of Canada's annual George Bernard Shaw Festivals. He is a frequent lecturer on literary and social topics for the Canadian Broadcasting Commission.

DENNIS WELLAND teaches English at the University of Manchester, England. He is the author of *Arthur Miller, Wilfred Owen,* and *The Pre-Raphaelites in Literature and Art,* and editor of Benjamin Franklin's *Autobiography and Other Pieces.* He also edits the *Journal of American Studies* for the British Association of American Studies.

Selected Bibliography

Readers are referred to the several essays in this volume taken from fuller original texts. See also the works listed in footnotes to the Introduction and the following essays:

Bentley, Eric. "The Innocence of Arthur Miller." In Bentley, *What Is Theatre? Incorporating "The Dramatic Event" and Other Reviews 1944–1967.* New York: Athenaeum Press, 1968, pp. 62–65. Miller's "unreconstructed liberalism" insists on the complete innocence of Proctor, thus reducing *The Crucible* to melodrama.

Bergeron, David M. "Arthur Miller's *The Crucible* and Nathaniel Hawthorne: Some Parallels." *English Journal,* 58 (January 1969), 47–55. Deals principally with *The Scarlet Letter.*

Eisenstatt, Martha T. "Arthur Miller: a Bibliography." *Modern Drama,* 5 (May 1962), 93–106.

Fender, Stephen. "Precision and Pseudo-Precision in *The Crucible.*" *Journal of American Studies,* 1 (1967), 87–98. The phony language of the play's orthodox Puritans reveals a society without moral referents; Proctor constructs a consistent moral system by giving Salem a viable language.

Hayashi, Tetsumaro. *Arthur Miller Criticism, 1930–1967.* Metuchen, N.J.: The Scarecrow Press, 1969. A bibliography.

Levin, David. "Salem Witchcraft in Recent Fiction and Drama." *New England Quarterly,* 28 (December 1955), 537–46. Mixes praise with his contention that Miller misunderstands the Puritan social and legal system, and distorts history.

Miller, Arthur. "Journey to *The Crucible.*" *The New York Times,* February 8, 1953, II, p. 3. Interesting account of Miller's visit to Salem to read trial records.

Nelson, Benjamin. "Because It Is My Name!" In Nelson, *Arthur Miller: Portrait of a Playwright*. New York: David McKay Company, 1970, pp. 146–74. Lengthy, rather general analysis of most of the usual topics.

Rovere, Richard. "Arthur Miller's Conscience." *New Republic*, 136 (June 17, 1957), 13–15. Reprinted in Rovere, *The American Establishment and Other Reports, Opinions and Speculations*. New York: Harcourt Brace Jovanovich, Inc., 1962, pp. 276–84. Compares Proctor's and Miller's refusal to "inform," and argues that this scrupulosity of the modern conscience could lead to the collapse of the machinery of law enforcement.

Walker, Phillip. "Arthur Miller's *The Crucible*: Tragedy or Allegory?" *Western Speech*, 20 (Fall 1956), 222–24. Though *The Crucible* tries to be both personal tragedy and political allegory it is actually neither, because the two genres are incompatible and cancel each other.

Warshow, Robert. "The Liberal Conscience in *The Crucible*." *Commentary*, 15 (March 1953), 265–71. Reprinted in Warshow, *The Immediate Experience*. New York: Doubleday, 1962, pp. 189–203. Devastating attack on Miller's alleged intellectual evasions on the McCarthy issue.

Watts, Richard, Jr. "Introduction." In Arthur Miller, *The Crucible*. New York: Bantam, 1959, pp. ix–xiv. *The Crucible* is a modern morality play that grows in stature the more its audiences appreciate the validity of Miller's analysis of mass pressures for intellectual conformity.